# The Wayland Library of Science and Technology

# THE CHANGING LANDSCAPE

## DOUGAL DIXON

Wayland

# The Wayland Library of Science and Technology

The Nature of Matter
The Universal Forces
Stars and Galaxies
The Solar System
The Changing Landscape
Air and Oceans
Origins of Life
The Science of Life
Plants and Animals
Animal Behaviour
The Human Machine
Health and Medicine

The Environment
Feeding the World
Raw Materials
Manufacturing Industry
Energy Sources
The Power Generators
Transport
Space Travel
Communications
The Computer Age
Scientific Instruments
Towards Tomorrow

**Advisory Series Editor**
Robin Kerrod

**Consultants**
Professor D.C. Imrie, Dr J. Beynon

**Editor:** Steve Luck
**Designer:** David West · Children's Book Design
**Production:** Steve Elliott
**Art Director:** John Ridgeway
**Project Director:** Lawrence Clarke

First published in 1990 by
Wayland (Publishers) Ltd
61 Western Road, Hove
East Sussex BN3 1JD, England

AN EQUINOX BOOK

Planned and produced by:
Equinox (Oxford) Limited
Musterlin House, Jordan Hill Road,
Oxford OX2 8DP

**British Library Cataloguing in Publication Data**

Dixon, Dougal
The Changing Landscape
1. Earth. Structure and physical properties
I. Title
551.1
ISBN 1-85210-890-8

Media conversion and typesetting by Peter
MacDonald, Una Macnamara and Vanessa Hersey
Origination by Hong Kong Reprohouse Co Ltd
Printed in Italy by Rotolito Lombarda
S.p.A., Milan
Bound in France by AGM

**Front cover:** The Grand Canyon in Arizona
in the United States.
**Back cover:** The formation of continents.

# Contents

# Introduction

The Earth was born from a cloud of dust and gas nearly 5 billion years ago, along with the other planets in our Solar System. But the Earth evolved quite differently from the others, making it possible for life to flourish in a myriad of different forms.

From the time that the Earth cooled and formed a solid crust, it has been ever changing. Even as the rocks and mountains formed, the weather and other agents set to work to grind them down. Huge continents formed and they began to split up under the action of relentless forces deep inside the crust.

Such elemental forces are still at work today, creating and demolishing mountains, and setting the Earth quaking and volcanoes erupting. The investigation of such forces forms part of one of the most exciting of all the sciences, geology, the study of the Earth.

◀ The Grand Canyon in Arizona in the United States. The Canyon was formed over 26 million years ago. It has a maximum depth of some 2,080 m from the plateau top to the Colorado River.

# The planet Earth

The Earth, our home planet, is quite unlike any other in the Solar System. It was formed at the same time as the rest of the Solar System. It is a rocky planet like Mercury, Venus and Mars, the other inner planets. However, the Earth's distance from the Sun gives it the conditions that can allow water to exist and first enabled life to develop. The Earth spins on its axis and moves around the Sun. These motions give us, respectively, days and years. The tilt of its axis creates the seasons. Modern scientific techniques allow us both to investigate the Earth's interior, and to survey the surface of the planet.

▶ Steam arises above an area of geysers and hot springs. These occur in volcanic regions where the Earth's outer skin, or crust, is weak or the forces underneath are very strong.

# The unique Earth

The Sun is at the centre of a whole family of planets. Close to it are the inner planets – Mercury, Venus, Earth and Mars.

Mercury, closest to the Sun, is an airless, cratered rock not much larger than our Moon. It is a blisteringly hot cinder of a world totally incapable of supporting life of any kind. If it once had an atmosphere, this would have disappeared into space long ago.

Venus is the next planet out from the Sun and is about the same size as the Earth. Whereas Mercury is airless, Venus is clothed in a thick atmosphere of mainly carbon dioxide. At the surface, the pressure of the atmosphere is nearly 100 times that of Earth. The thick blanket of gases acts like a greenhouse and traps the Sun's heat, and gives a surface temperature as high as 480°C. There can be no life on Venus.

Mars, the planet beyond us, is smaller than the Earth. Mars also has an atmosphere, but only a very low pressure one. Again, the atmosphere consists largely of carbon dioxide.

Water exists on the surface, but only in the form of ice at the poles. Pressures and temperatures are never high enough to make all the ice melt. The whole planet is a red, lifeless desert.

Beyond Mars lie the outer planets – the gas giants of Jupiter, Saturn, Uranus and Neptune. These are far larger than the Earth, and their outer visible structure consists of the gases hydrogen and helium. They are so unlike the Earth and the other inner planets, in structure and composition, that it is difficult to make comparisons. Beyond them, the outermost planet Pluto is so distant that it is something of a mystery altogether.

Among all the planets, only the Earth is of such a size and at such a distance from the Sun that its surface is neither too cold nor too hot. Because of the temperature and pressure, water can exist in all its three forms – as gas, liquid and solid. These conditions also allow plants and animals to reproduce and evolve. In short, Earth is the only planet that has the conditions that support life.

▲ Photographs sent back from the Martian surface by the *Viking* space probes in 1976 showed a red stony desert with a red dusty sky. No sign of life was found. The low temperatures and pressures make Mars very unsuitable for living things.

◄ The Earth has blue skies filled with clouds, and in most places there is standing or running water. Life abounds, with plants using sunlight and water to make food. Plants in turn support the complex web of animal life across the globe.

# Earth's origins

Since the dawn of history people have wondered about how the Earth came to exist. Many theories were put forward, based on what little knowledge was available at the time. Most of these are now out of date. Nowadays, with the use of modern technology, we are continually amassing more and more information about the Solar System and how the Earth was born. We use satellites, space probes and scientific instruments to look at the stars and the planets. We are gradually finding out what makes the stars give out light and what the planets are made of. Scientists use this knowledge to find out more about our own Earth.

The most up-to-date theory suggests that the whole Solar System – the Sun, the Earth and the rest of the planets, moons and asteroids – formed from a single mass of cold dust and gas called a nebula. About 4,600 million years ago the nebula began to shrink. This was caused by the force of gravity, which pulls objects together because of their mass.

While this process continued, the Sun began to form. As it shrank, the nebula began to spin, which made it flatten out into a disc. The spinning at the centre was greater than towards the outside of the disc, and the outermost parts sheared off as rings. The material at the centre heated up rapidly, and then began to shine as the Sun.

The planets could have formed when the gas and dust in the rings gathered together into solid bodies. Or they may have been built up from layers of dust.

## Formation of the planets

There are two theories about how the Solar System may have formed. It probably started out as a nebula, consisting of clouds of dust and gas, which contracted to form the Sun and planets. According to the accretion theory (1), the force of gravity caused lumps of matter to become welded together. They grew into larger and larger bodies until they became planets. The alternative proto-planet theory (2) suggests that dust from the nebula gathered in various gravitational centres and then gathered together to form the planets.

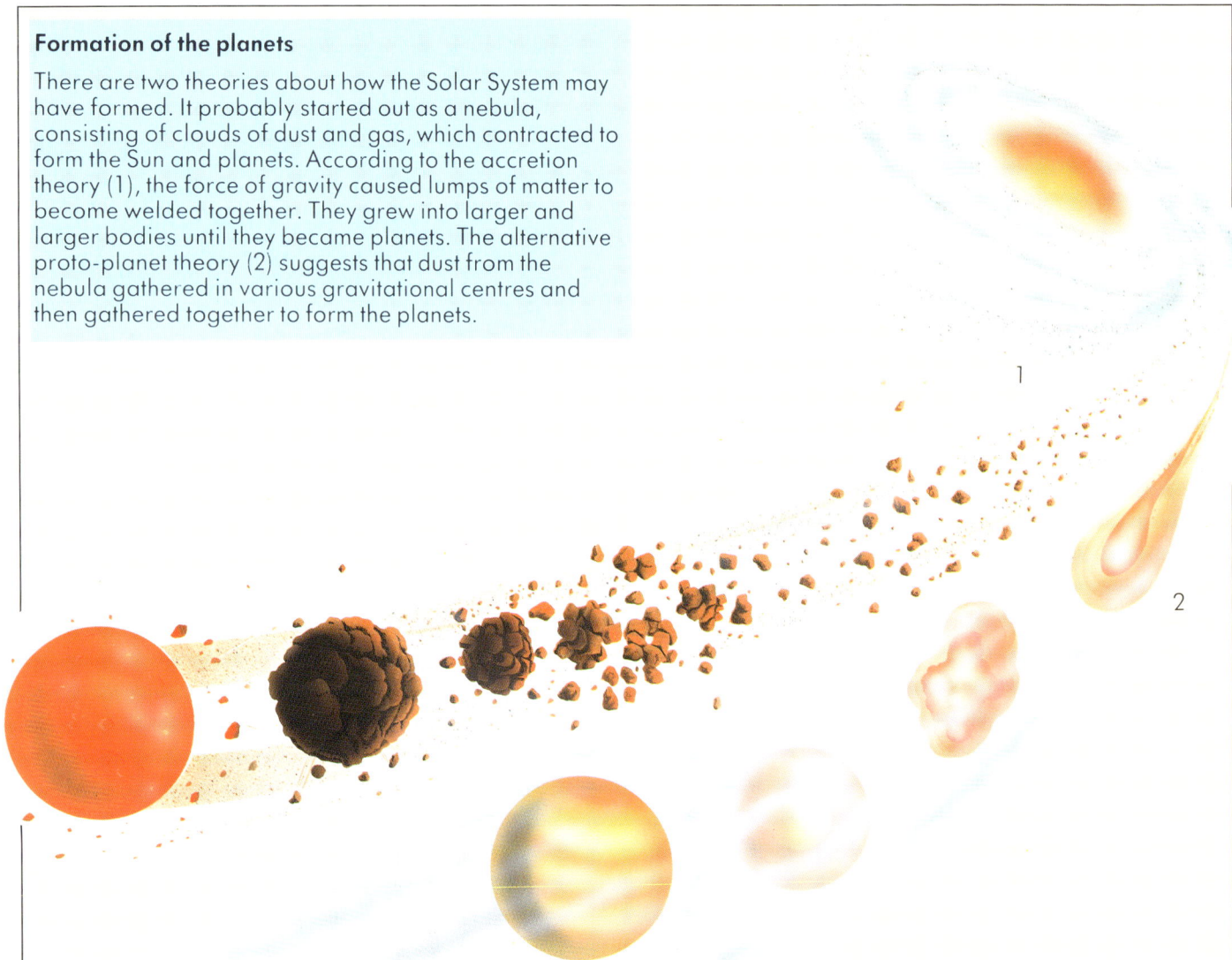

# Gravity and magnetism

A tremendous force caused the original nebula to contract and form the Solar System. This was the force of gravity. It is difficult to define, but it acts on all matter in the Universe. Its effect is to pull towards each other all things that have mass – planets, rocks or particles of dust. The gravitational force between the Earth and all of the objects on the Earth causes the objects to have weight.

Other major effects result from the Earth's magnetic field. The Earth acts like a giant magnet, tending to pull magnetic materials towards its north and south poles. This effect is used in a compass, which points northwards because the magnetic north pole is near the geographical North Pole. The origin of the magnetic field may be the Earth's core.

▲ The Aurora Borealis, or Northern Lights, occurs when the Earth's magnetic field traps charged particles from the Sun. The particles interact with molecules in the air and make them give off a glow.

## Earth's magnetic field

The magnetic field of the Earth resembles that of a giant magnet in the centre of the Earth, pointing north and south. A compass (below) has a magnetized needle pivoted at its centre so that it can swing from side to side. The right-hand side of the diagram (below right) shows how a compass needle lines itself up with the magnetic field. As a result, it always points to the north. The magnetic and geographic poles are usually in slightly different places. A dip needle is a magnetic needle pivoted so that it can swing up and down. It also follows the magnetic field lines, and points straight up or straight down when over the poles.

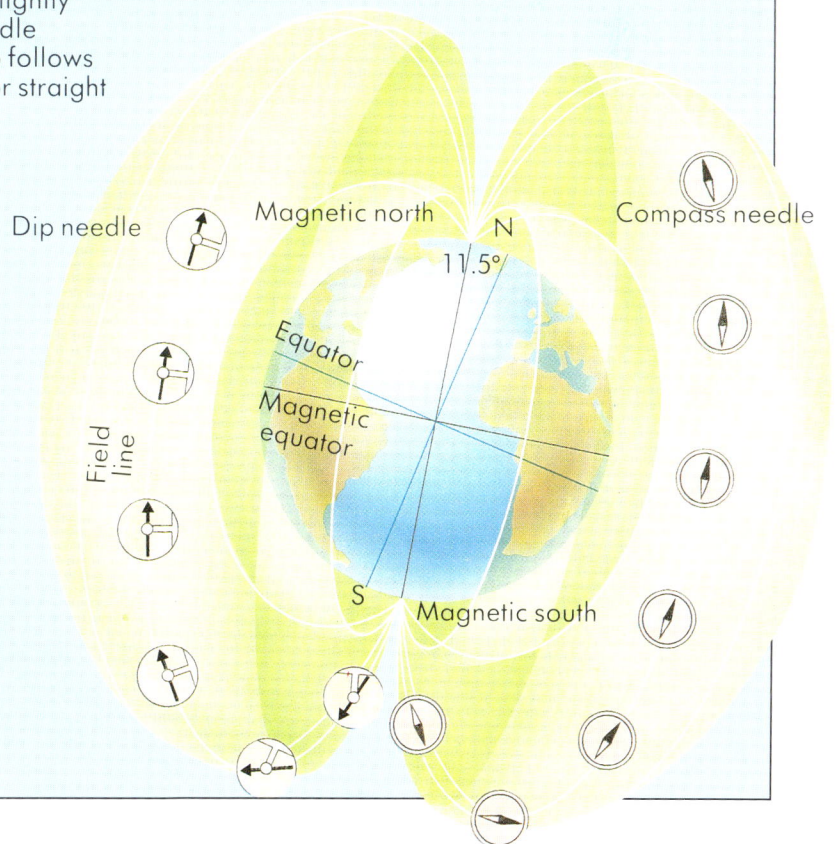

Dip needle · Magnetic north · N · 11.5° · Compass needle · Equator · Magnetic equator · Field line · S · Magnetic south

# The skin of the Earth

The Earth's surface is in constant motion. It is made up of a series of slabs, or "plates", which shift and drift so slowly that the movement can hardly be detected. Yet over millions of years we can see the result as continental drift – the gradual movement of the continents.

The moving part of the Earth is a stiff skin, the lithosphere, about 75 km thick. It lies on top of a softer layer called the asthenosphere. The lithosphere is like a cooling scum forming on the more plastic asthenosphere.

▶ A cross-section of the Earth shows weak points where material from the asthenosphere pushes to the surface to form new lithosphere. They occur on ridges along the ocean floor, as in the Indian Ocean Rise (1).

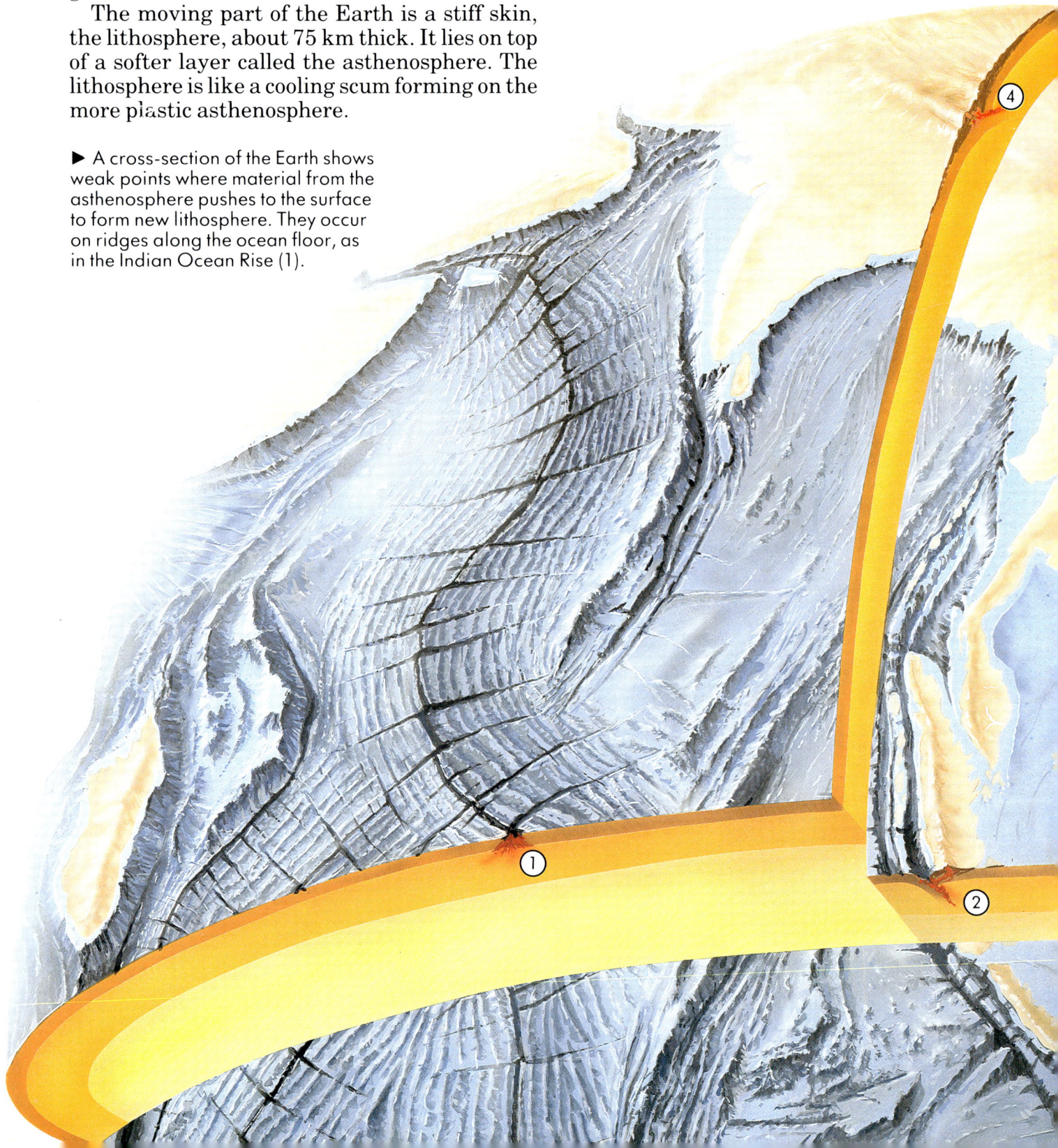

▼ Deep ocean trenches occur within the Earth's crust, such as along the edge of the East Indies. Or there are great mountain ranges, such as the Himalayas (4). All this activity splits the Earth's surface into a series of moving plates. The whole process has been given the name plate tectonics. At constructive plate margins (1), molten material wells up from the Earth's interior. There it cools and solidifies to form new lithosphere. At destructive plate margins (2, 3 and 4), the old lithosphere is swallowed up and destroyed. A subduction zone forms, where one plate slides down beneath another. The edges of continents may crumple up here into mountain ranges.

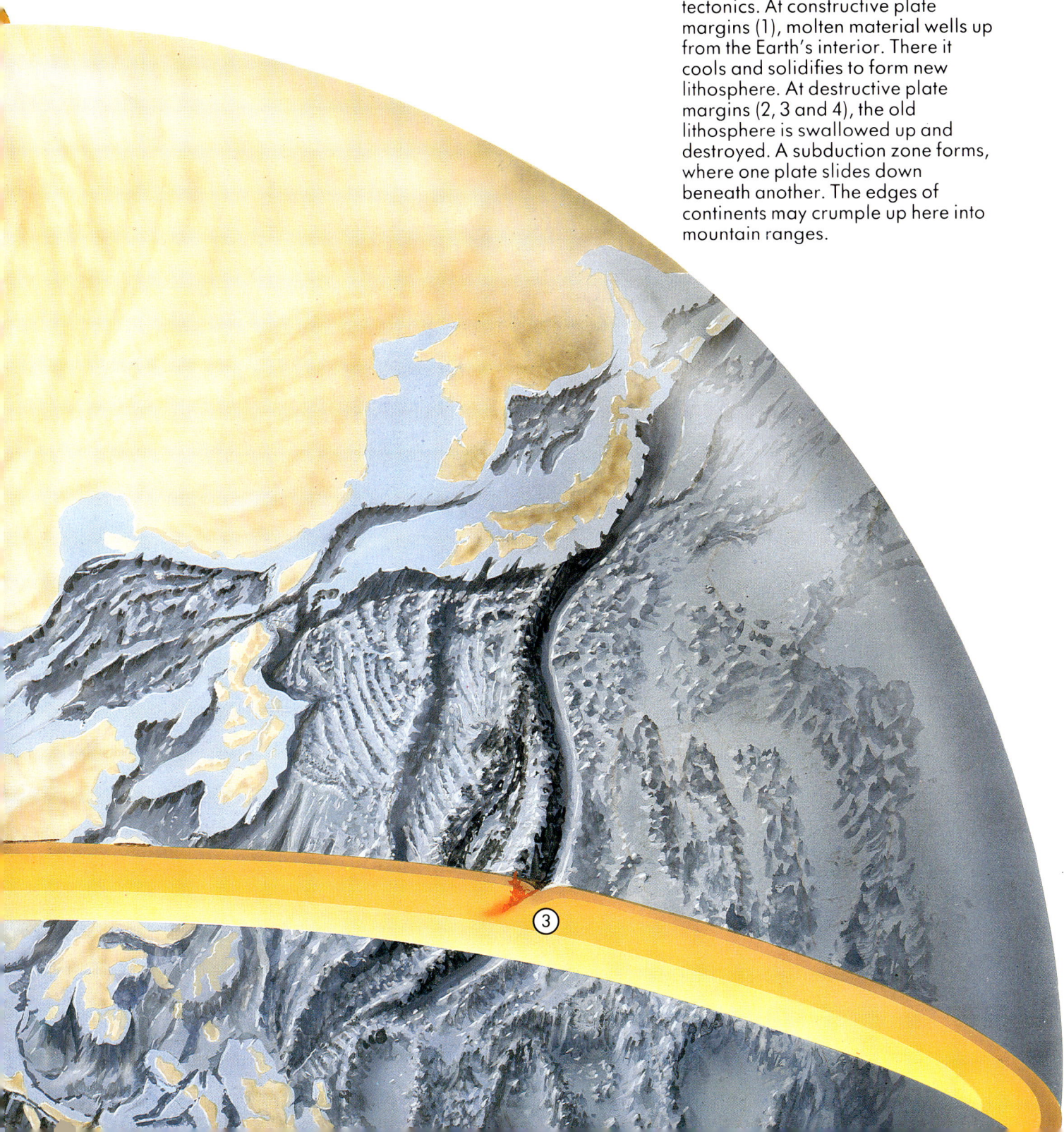

③

# Earth's motion

At one stage when the Solar System was forming, the planets were nothing more than a series of rings of loose particles around the early Sun. It was gravitational force that held the particles in each ring. They were being pulled inwards towards the Sun, but at the same time they were moving along so fast that they were flying past it. At a certain speed the two movements balanced and the particles fell into orbit round the Sun, never reaching it but never breaking away. An orbit is a circular or elliptical path in which the tendency of a body to fly away into space is just balanced by the force of gravity pulling it inwards.

When the rings solidifed into the planets, the planets themselves were still in orbit around the Sun. Many of them had smaller bodies in orbit around them. These are known as satellites or moons.

The Earth's orbit is not circular, but is slightly elliptical. At its closest point to the Sun (perihelion) it comes to within 147,100,000 km. At its farthest point (aphelion) it is 152,100,000 km away. The Earth reaches perihelion in early January, and aphelion in July. It takes 365¼ days for the Earth to travel once round its orbit. This is the period of time we call a year.

As the Earth travels in its elliptical orbit, it also spins, or rotates, on its own axis. It does this every 24 hours, giving us our days and nights. The Earth's axis is tilted at an angle (23½°) to the plane of its orbit round the Sun. At perihelion the North Pole is tilted away from the Sun and the South Pole tilted towards it. At aphelion the tilt is reversed, the South Pole tilting away from the Sun and the North Pole tilting towards it. It is the tilt which gives rise to the change of seasons throughout the world.

## Changing seasons

It is the tilt of the Earth's axis that creates the various seasons. The Earth's axis is tilted at 23½° to the plane of its orbit around the Sun. As the North Pole tilts towards the Sun in June, the Sun does not set at all in the far north, and it is northern summer. It is northern winter when the North Pole tilts away from the Sun.

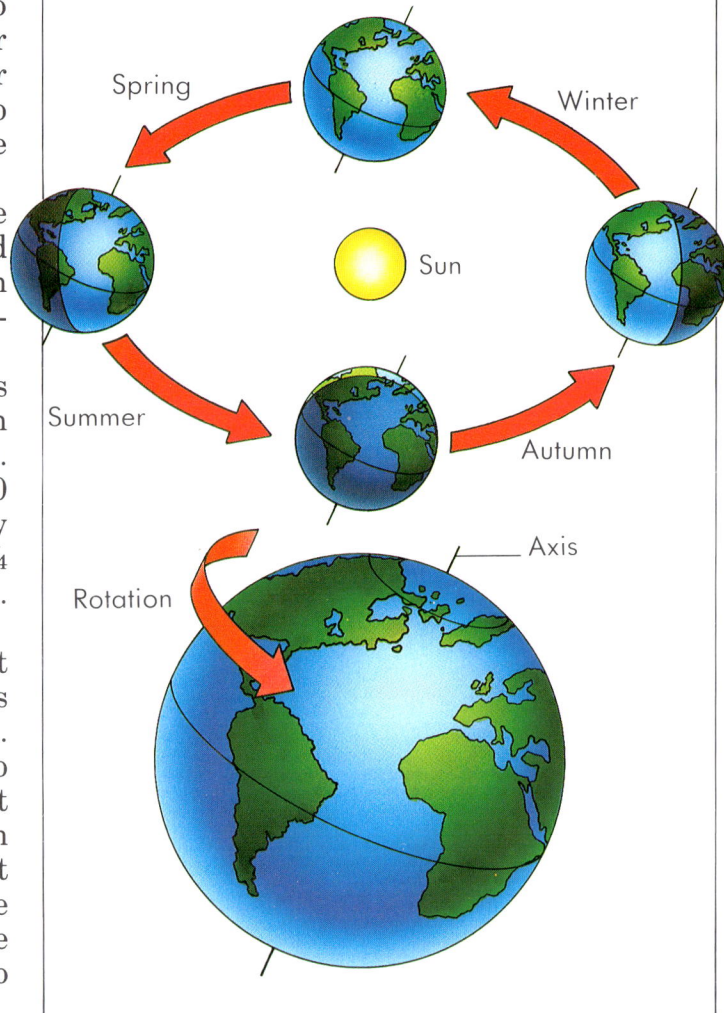

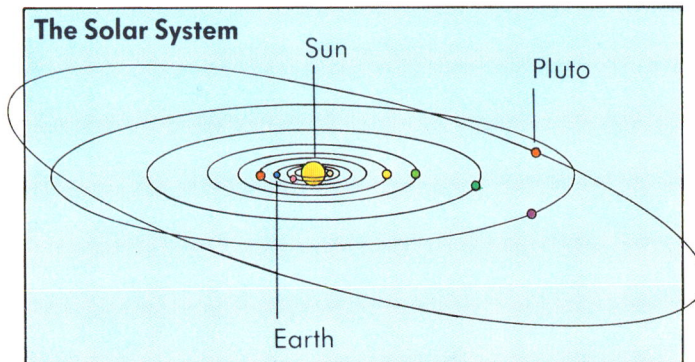

Spring

Winter

Sun

Summer

Autumn

Axis

Rotation

## The Solar System

Sun

Pluto

Earth

◀ The orbits of nearly all the planets of the Solar System lie in much the same plane. This would have been the plane of the original disc of gas that formed the Solar System. A notable exception is Pluto, which has an orbit that is tilted in relation to this plane. Pluto's orbit is also highly elliptical, and at its perihelion the planet actually lies inside Neptune's orbit.

▼ When seen from space, the Earth looks perfectly round. The deepest ocean basins and the highest mountains hardly blemish its spherical surface. But the Earth is slightly flattened at the North and South Poles. As the Earth spins on its axis, the rotation makes it bulge outwards along the Equator.

# Structure of the Earth

As the Earth solidifed from its nebula of gas and dust, its components separated themselves according to their densities. Perhaps the densest substances congregated first, and then the less dense ones gathered on the outside. This would have resulted in a structure with a heavy central core and a lighter covering. Alternatively, all the substances may have clumped together at the same time. Then the densest of them would have sunk through to collect at the centre. Whatever happened, we now have a planet with a massive core covered by a number of different layers.

At the centre lies the core. It is made of the heavy metals iron and nickel. There are two layers here. The inner core is solid, whereas the outer core is liquid.

Around the core lies the rocky mantle, which also consists of two layers. The mantle makes up the bulk of the Earth. It is mostly solid and is made of silicates, compounds of silicon and oxygen. Most of the Earth's rocks are made up of silicates.

On the outside is the crust. This is, to us, the most important of the layers, and it is the only one we can reach directly. There are two types of crust, made of slightly different silicate materials. The larger area consists of oceanic crust, which is quite thin. It is made largely of silica and magnesium, and is given the shorthand name sima. The second type of crust forms the continents. It is made mostly of silica and aluminium, and is called sial.

Sial is lighter and thicker than sima. The continents are formed of separate lumps of sial "floating" in the sima of the ocean floor. Unlike the sima, the sial is not carried downwards. As a result, the continents are much older than the ocean floors.

The layers of lithosphere and asthenosphere, which make up and move the plates of the Earth's surface, are found towards the outside of the globe. The solid lithosphere consists of the crust and the uppermost part of the mantle. The soft asthenosphere is a distinct layer of mantle positioned just below it.

▼ Pillow lavas are found on the seabed. They are cushion-shaped lumps of volcanic material formed when lava erupts from a submerged ocean ridge and cools quickly. The whole of the deep ocean floor, beneath the sediments, is formed of pillow lavas. They are part of the sima – the material of the oceanic crust. Sima is rarely seen because it lies beneath several kilometres of ocean water and sediments.

▼ All the minerals and rocks of mountains and plains are components of the sial. The sial – the material of the continental crust – is all around us. It tends to be more complex than the sima, because it is much older. Its rocks are constantly being lifted up by mountain-building activity and worn away by weather and rivers. The fragments are redeposited as sediments, and eventually they are turned into solid rocks once more.

**Earth's layers**

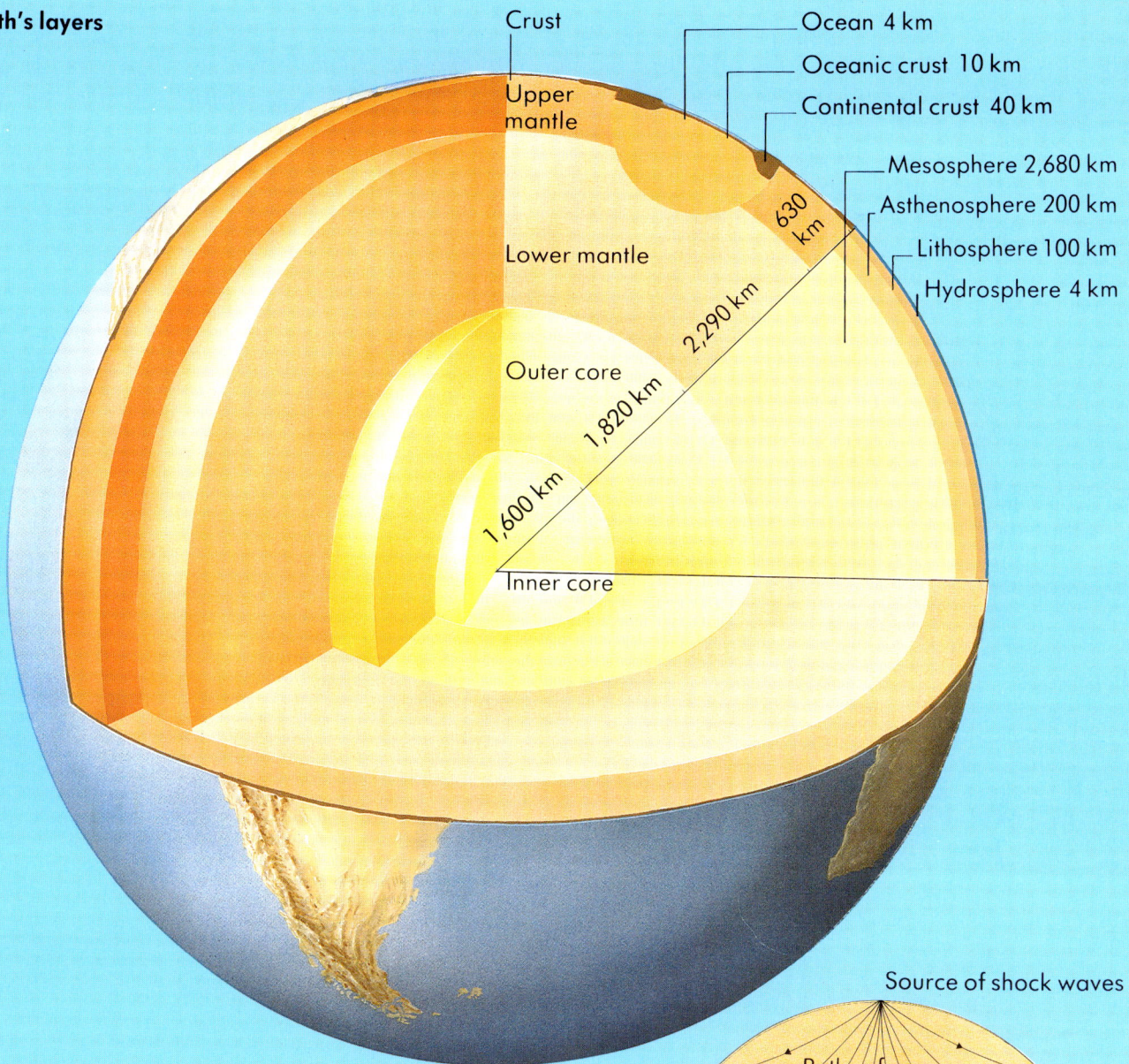

Crust

Ocean 4 km

Oceanic crust 10 km

Continental crust 40 km

Upper mantle

Mesosphere 2,680 km

Asthenosphere 200 km

Lower mantle

Lithosphere 100 km

Hydrosphere 4 km

630 km

2,290 km

1,820 km

Outer core

1,600 km

Inner core

Source of shock waves

Paths of waves

Inner core

Outer core

Mantle

▲ A thin solid crust forms the top layer of the Earth. With the solid upper part of the mantle, it makes up the lithosphere. Underneath is a softer layer of mantle, the asthenosphere, on which the "plates" of the lithosphere can move. The mesosphere is the main part of the mantle. At the Earth's centre is the core. The outer part is liquid; the inner part, solid.

▶ Geologists investigate the structure of the Earth by studying the paths of shock waves through it. The shock waves may be set off naturally by earthquakes or artificially by explosions. This picture shows the paths of the primary (P), or compression waves. Note how they bend when they pass from one layer to another.

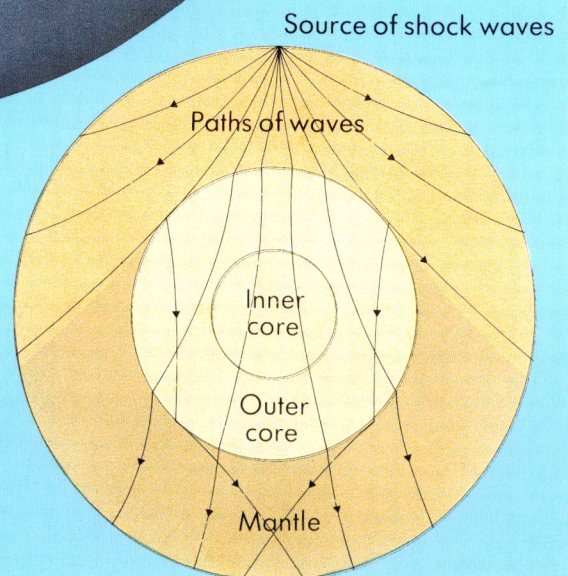

# Continents adrift

The surface of the Earth is an unstable, shifting place. Since the mid-1960s it has been known that the crust and the topmost layer of the mantle form a number of distinct plates that cover the Earth like the panels of a football. The plates are being generated continuously along one edge and destroyed along another. The shifting of continents across the globe, something suspected for centuries, is the result of all this movement. Earthquakes and volcanic eruptions are two destructive side-effects that occur at plate boundaries.

► The Himalayas are the highest mountain range on Earth. They were formed quite recently – within the last 50 million years – by the northward movement of the plate that carries India.

# Dynamic Earth

The greatest mountain ranges on Earth – the Himalayas, Rockies, Andes, Alps and Urals – were formed by a folding action of the upper layers of the Earth's crust. As a result, the rocks are twisted and bent, obviously deformed under some great pressure. It is the movement of the Earth's surface plates – the action of plate tectonics – that has brought this about.

Each plate is created from molten material from the Earth's interior. This wells up in volcanic activity along the great ridges that run along the ocean beds. The plates build out from their edges and move apart. Eventually, when a plate meets another plate travelling in the opposite direction, one plate slides beneath the other and is destroyed.

Sometimes this destructive plate margin lies along the edge of a continent, as it does along the western coast of South America. Then the edge of the continent is crumpled up into a mountain range – in this instance the Andes. Often two continents collide and produce a range where the two continents have fused. The Himalayas and Urals formed in this way.

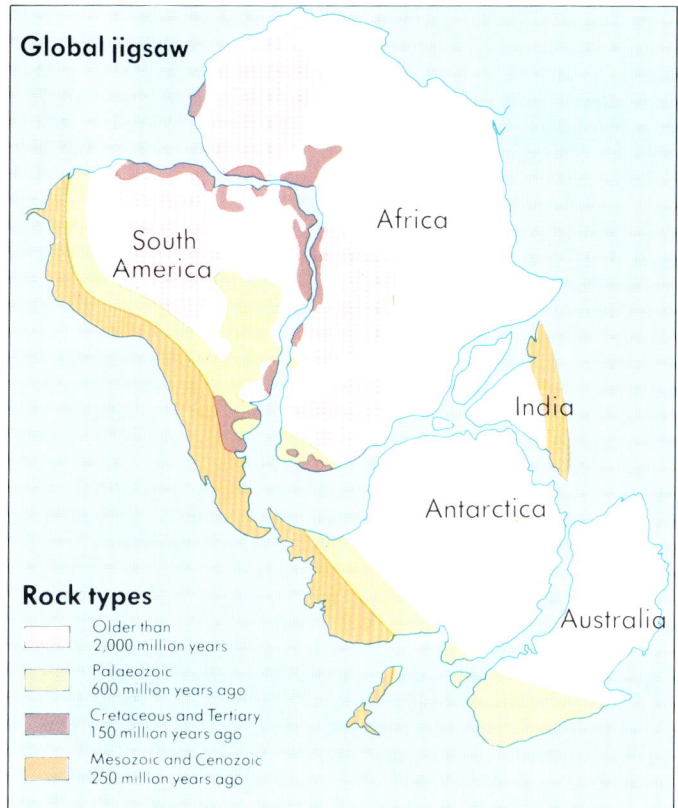

**Global jigsaw**

South America

Africa

India

Antarctica

Australia

**Rock types**

Older than 2,000 million years

Palaeozoic 600 million years ago

Cretaceous and Tertiary 150 million years ago

Mesozoic and Cenozoic 250 million years ago

▲ Continents may split apart as new constructive plate margins develop beneath them. South America, Africa, India, Antarctica and Australia were once a single landmass. They broke up and drifted apart as new oceanic crust developed between them. We know this because of the shapes of the continental shelves, the similarity of fossils on each landmass, the continuation of mountain ranges across them and similar rock types.

◄ The intensely folded rocks of Wales are the result of past movements. Once there was another ocean where the Atlantic now lies. This closed up as the landmasses on the east and west collided. They threw up a mountain range like the Himalayas. After many millions of years the continents broke apart again and the modern Atlantic Ocean formed between. The remains of the old mountain range lie in the Appalachians in North America, and the Welsh, Scottish and Norwegian highlands in Europe.

# Surface plates

In the 1960s, scientists studying the bottom of the Atlantic Ocean began to notice something that led to a revolution in geological knowledge. All rocks contain magnetic particles, and when they are formed, their magnetism lines up along the Earth's magnetic field. At the crest of the Mid-Atlantic Ridge, the ocean ridge that runs north to south along the Atlantic Ocean, the magnetism of the rocks lines up as expected. But to each side the rocks have a reversed magnetism, evidently produced at a time of magnetic reversal.

These magnetic reversals happen from time to time, when the Earth's magnetic North Pole and South Pole change polarity. Further exploration showed that down the sides of the ridge the rocks showed alternating stripes of normal and reversed magnetism. The pattern on one side was the mirror image of the pattern on the other. This indicates that the seabed is being created along the crest of the ridge, and is moving away to each side as new material continues to well up from below. As each band of new rock is formed, it lines up with the direction of the Earth's magnetic field at the time. This process is called seafloor spreading.

Further proof that the rocks of the seabed are spreading came when it was noticed that the rocks on the ridge of the crest are fresh, whereas those farther away are covered in sediment. The sediment layer becomes thicker even farther from the crest, reflecting how much older the seabed must be.

Soon this new concept of seafloor spreading was put together with the older discovery of continental drift to produce the new science called plate tectonics.

**The changing face of the Earth**

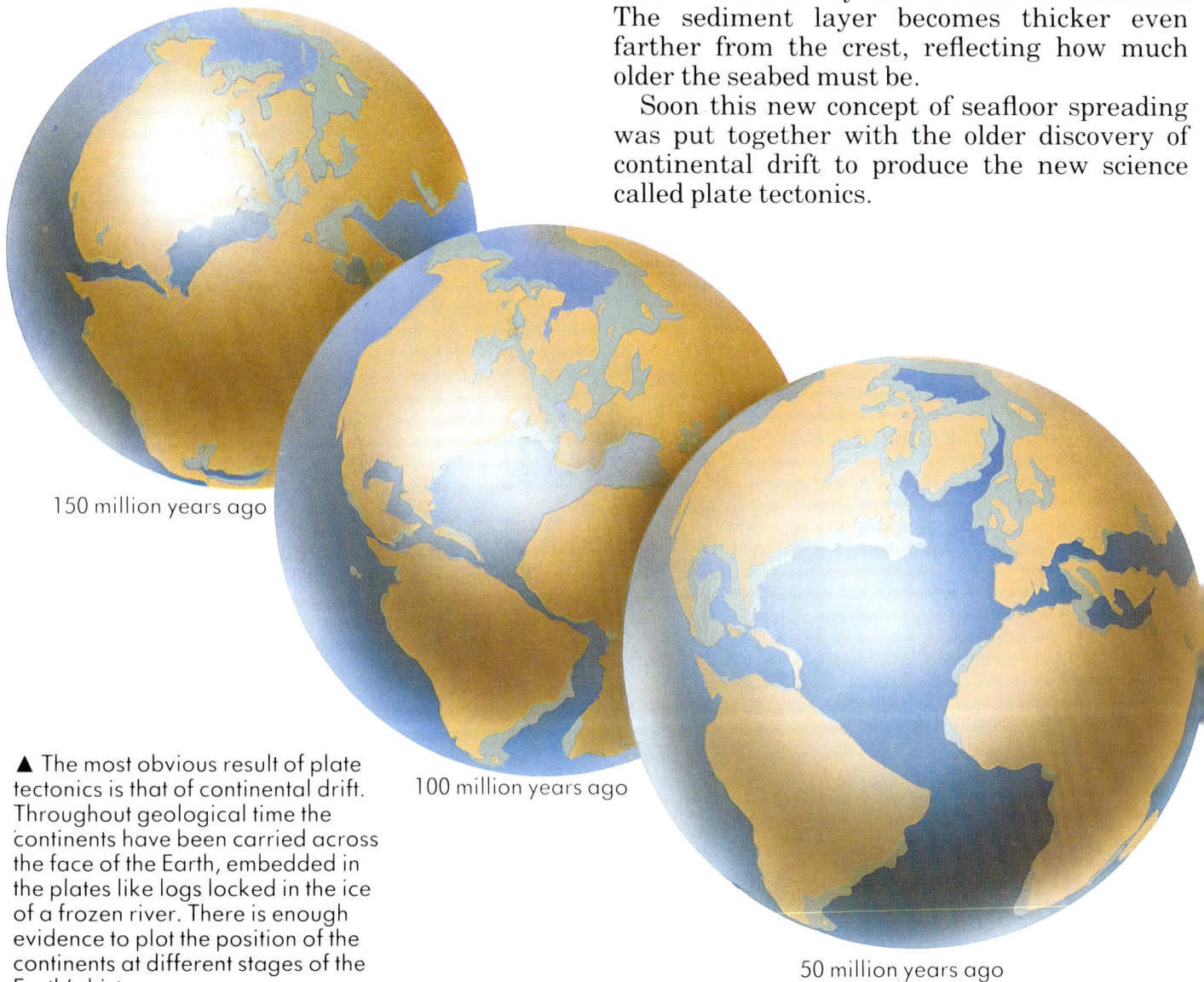

150 million years ago

100 million years ago

50 million years ago

▲ The most obvious result of plate tectonics is that of continental drift. Throughout geological time the continents have been carried across the face of the Earth, embedded in the plates like logs locked in the ice of a frozen river. There is enough evidence to plot the position of the continents at different stages of the Earth's history.

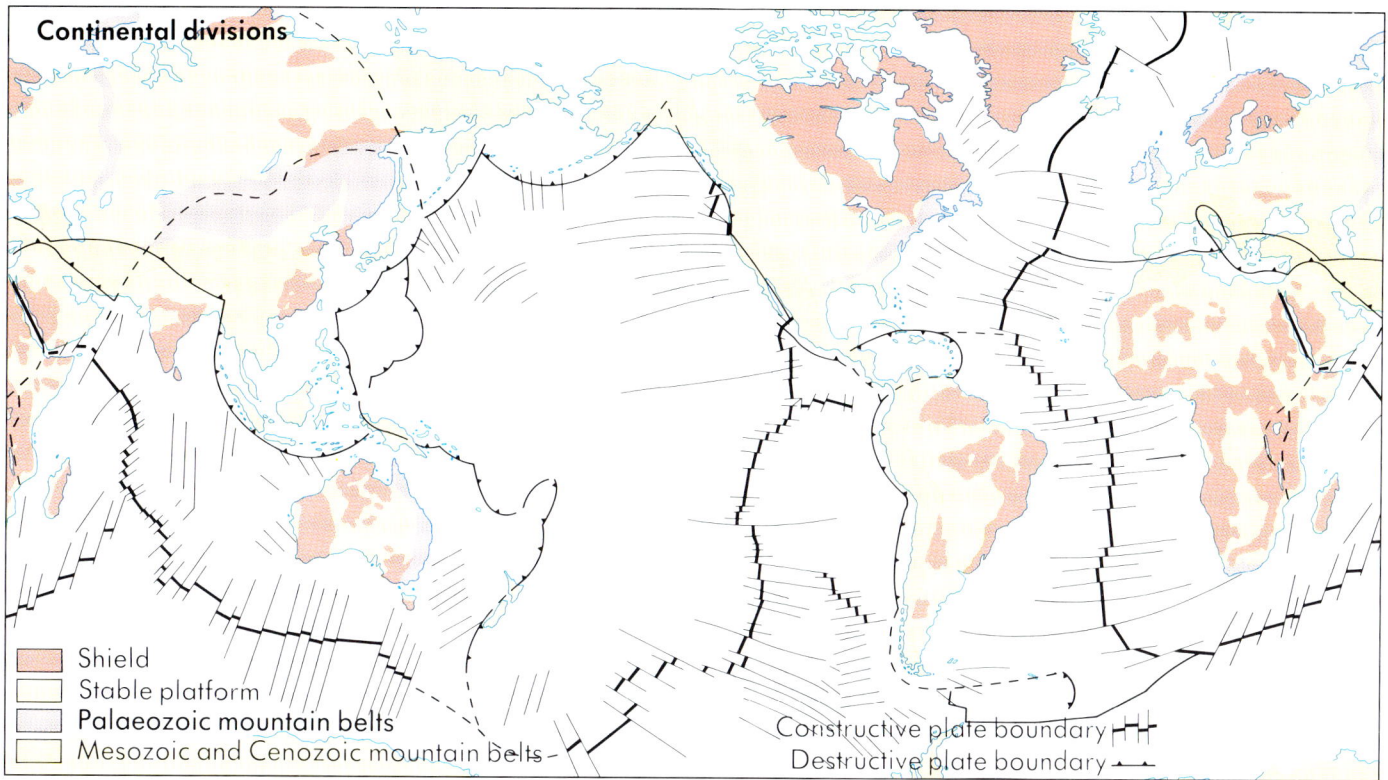

**Continental divisions**

Shield
Stable platform
Palaeozoic mountain belts
Mesozoic and Cenozoic mountain belts

Constructive plate boundary
Destructive plate boundary

▲ Continents are made up of three basic components: the shield, a flat plain of rock; the stable platforms, the base of which is made up of the same kind of rock as the shield, but with a layer of different rock on top; and the mountain belts. The oldest mountains – the Palaeozoic – are nearest the shield, and the younger – the Mesozoic and Cenozoic – are farthest away from it.

Today

**Wegener the pioneer**

In 1912 the German meteorologist Alfred Wegener (1880-1930) came up with the idea of continental drift based on sound scientific reasoning. He produced a series of maps of the world as it was in the past. They were essentially the same as those that can be produced today with our vastly increased knowledge. However, he could not account for the mechanics of the movement, and did not live to see plate tectonics provide the answer.

# Rifts and mountains

All the highlands and lowlands, mountain ranges and plains, and the whole large-scale landscape of the world today can be looked at as the result of the activity of plate tectonics.

The most extensive mountain ranges are those of the fold mountains. They are caused by compression – by two plates grinding into each other. When two plates, topped with oceanic crust, meet each other, one is destroyed. It slides down into the depths of the mantle, pulling down the seabed into an ocean trench, while the other plate rides up above it. As the descending plate melts, the molten material rises up through the overlying plate and bursts through to the surface as a series of volcanoes. These grow until they rise above the surface of the sea as an arc of volcanic islands. Many such island arcs, running parallel to ocean trenches,

are found along the northern and western fringes of the Pacific Ocean.

A slab of continental crust may be embedded in the oceanic crust of the plate that is being destroyed. Eventually this continent reaches the ocean trench at the subduction zone, and there the movement stops. Continental crust is too light to be drawn down into the mantle.

If the plate movement continues, the oceanic crust of the opposite plate then begins to slide down beneath the continent. This establishes another subduction zone and ocean trench. The edge of the continent deforms and crumples up with the activity, while sediments from the descending plate are scraped off against it. Molten material from below thrusts up through the continental edge and a series of volcanoes develops in the deformed margin. As a result, a

▶ When a continent begins to split apart, the action starts with the upwelling of material from the Earth's mantle (1). The continent above heaves upwards and splits into blocks. These may stand up as block mountains or subside as rift valleys. Molten material forces its way through the cracks (2). The sea floods in and the rift valley becomes a young ocean, with a floor of newly formed oceanic crust (3).

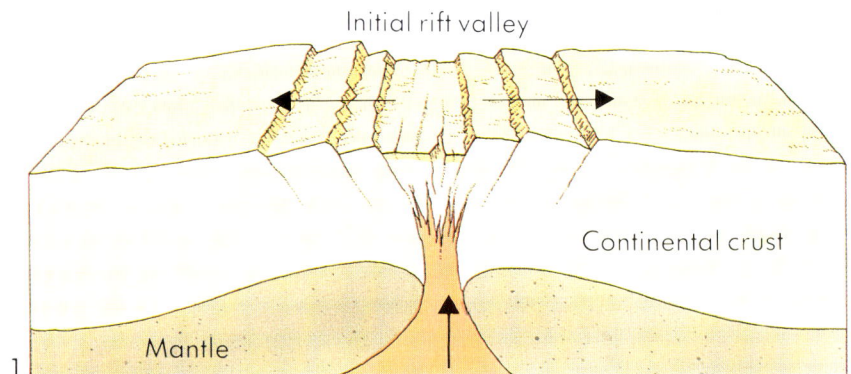

Initial rift valley

Continental crust

Mantle

1

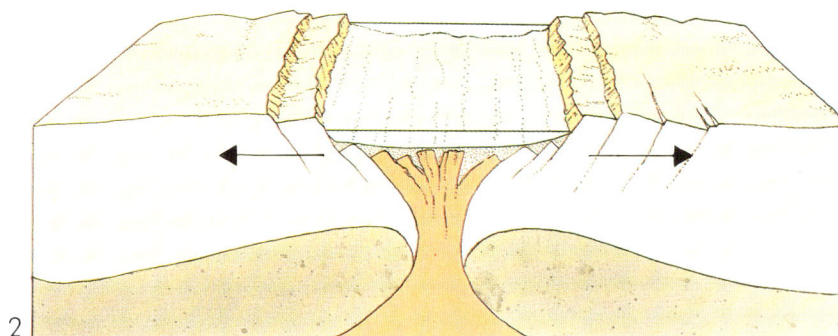

2

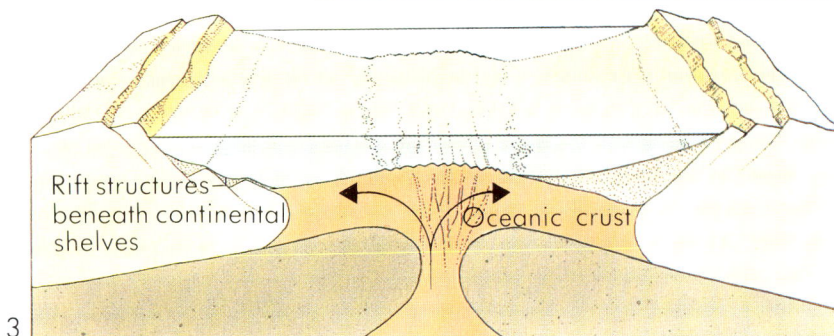

Rift structures beneath continental shelves

Oceanic crust

3

▶ The Great Rift Valley of eastern Africa shows where the African continent is being pulled apart. Farther north the valley's extension, the Red Sea, is already a young ocean.

very complex chain of fold mountains grows along the continental edge. The Andes, along the western edge of South America, are a particularly good example, with an ocean trench just offshore There are also a great number of volcanoes along their length, which is another typical feature of fold mountains.

The subducting plate may bring its own continent, and when the two collide the resulting mountain range is particularly enormous, such as the Himalayas between India and Asia. Now the movement really does stop. But the forces are still at work, and make themselves felt at some other part of the globe. A new constructive plate margin develops somewhere. If it is in the middle of a continent, the continent heaves up and cracks to produce the other major type of mountain range, the so-called block mountains.

As a result all the continents have the same general pattern. There is a central area of hard old rock, usually worn flat with age, surrounded by successively younger ranges of fold mountains. A rift valley among block mountains may show where the continent is being pulled apart. If one border of the continent shows the cracks and block mountains that we would associate with a rift valley, then the continent has probably broken away from another one some time in the past.

**Coastal volcanoes**

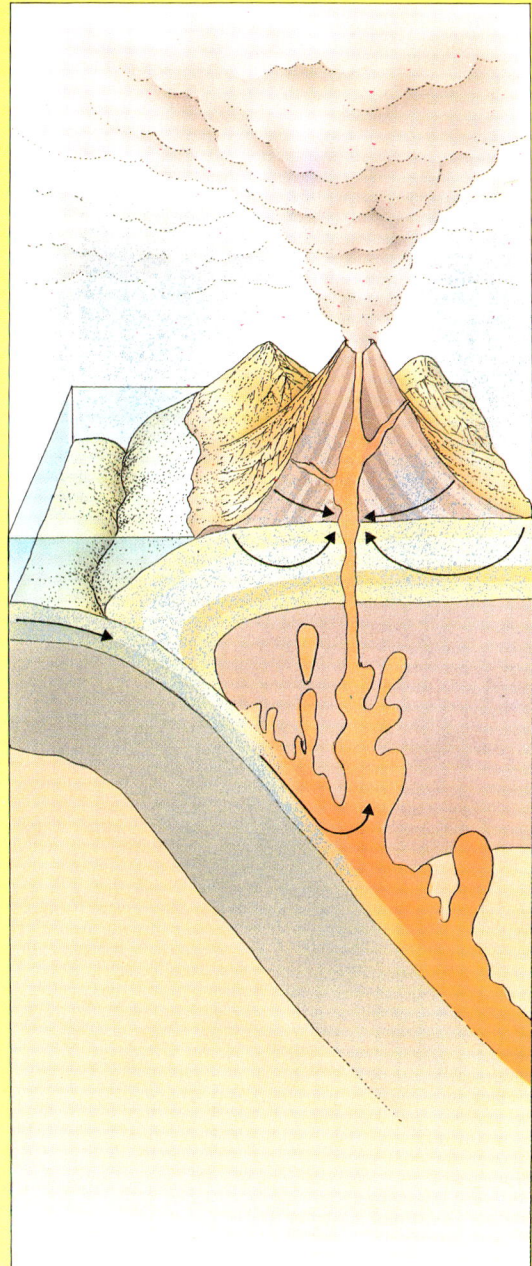

When one plate slides below the next, it is eventually destroyed in the mantle. Friction between the two plates melts the rock along the boundary, and this rises through the plate above, eventually forming volcanoes on the surface. The melting of the rocks is helped by the presence of seawater brought down by the moving plate, and a lot of water is erupted from the volcanoes.

# Volcanoes

Volcanoes occur where hot material leaks out from the Earth's interior. This usually happens at the margins of the tectonic plates.

At constructive plate margins, along the ocean ridges, the hot material from the mantle wells up and solidifies. The molten matter that is forced out at the surface is called lava. It solidifies not far from the vent, gradually building up into a mountain. The activity takes place on the ocean floor, and so these types of volcanoes are rarely seen. Only in places such as Iceland does the ocean ridge reach above the surface of the water. Then the volcanoes can be seen on land.

At destructive plate margins the molten material comes from the breakdown of the plates themselves, and the volcanoes form in island arcs or in fold mountains. The lava is a different type from constructive margin lava, and forms different types of volcanoes.

A third type of volcano is found away from the plate margin, over a "hot-spot" of activity deep in the mantle. The lava that erupts is of the same type as that found at a constructive plate margin, and the same kind of volcanoes are thereby produced.

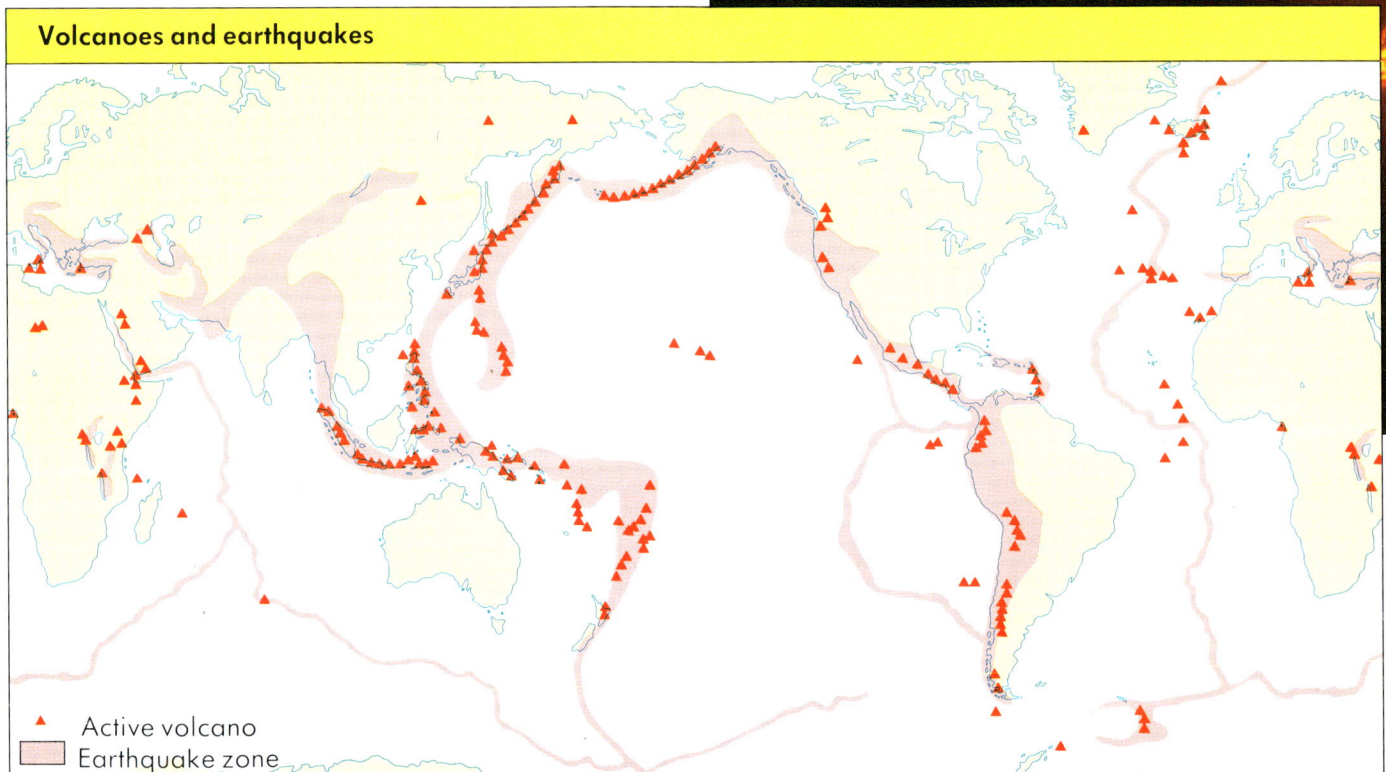

## Volcanoes and earthquakes

▲ Active volcano

Earthquake zone

## Types of volcanoes

At destructive plate margins the lava is rich in silica. This makes it stiff, producing steep-sided volcanoes such as the composite cones and cinder cones. Eruptions can be very violent, and the rock formed is called andesite. At constructive plate margins the lava contains less silica. It is runny and erupts quietly, producing broad shield volcanoes and fissures. The rocks that form are called basalts.

Composite volcano

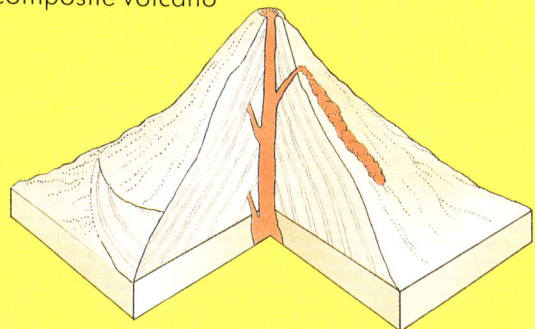

Cinder cone

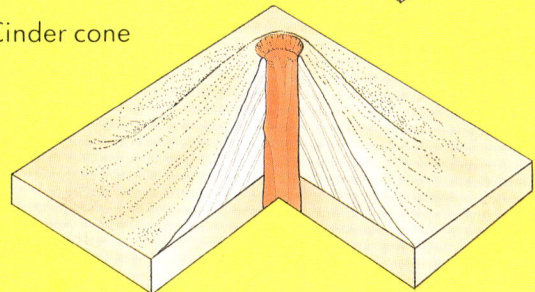

Shield volcano

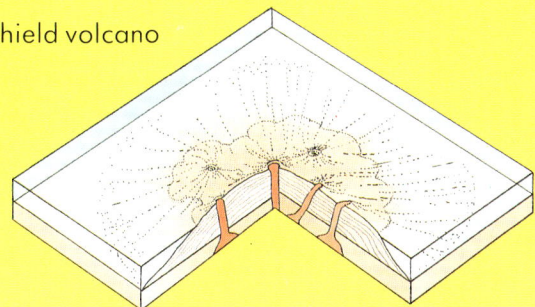

Fissure

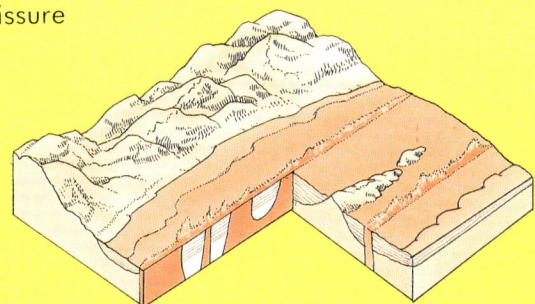

▲ A river of lava pours out from an erupting volcano. It is formed from magma from the mantle. As the magma rises and cools, some of its minerals solidify and sink back. Gases are given off as bubbles. The resulting lava does not have the same composition as the mantle.

◄ Most of the world's volcanoes are found along the margins of the plates. This distribution, as well as the distribution of earthquakes, shows where most of the plate tectonic activity is taking place.

# Earthquakes

Through the action of plate tectonics the crust of our planet is always moving. Over millions of years the continents drift from one place to another. They jostle together and push up mountain ranges. The movements do not take place continuously, but in small jerks and jumps. It is these jumps that set up the vibrations we call earthquakes.

The forces that sometimes move the crust of the Earth work all the time, and cause stresses to be built up in the rocks. Eventually the stresses become so strong that they make the rocks snap. They whip along a crack, called a fault, and this movement causes an earthquake shock. The shock waves travel outwards from the focus, the point where most of the movement takes place, like the ripples from a splash in a pond. The point on the Earth's surface directly above the focus is called the epicentre. Most damage is usually done there.

When the pieces of the Earth's crust snap along a fault, they usually move too far. Later they may spring back some distance and produce aftershocks, and this may continue until the rock masses have settled. Then the stresses begin to build up once more until they are released by the next earthquake.

The different types of shock wave produced by an earthquake travel at different speeds. Observatories around the world can detect them with instruments called seismographs. By timing when waves arrive, scientists can tell how far away the earthquake was. A world network of observatories can now pinpoint any earthquake's focus.

The places most likely to have earthquakes are the edges of the Earth's surface plates, where the plates are jostling each other and being created or destroyed. But earthquakes cannot be predicted.

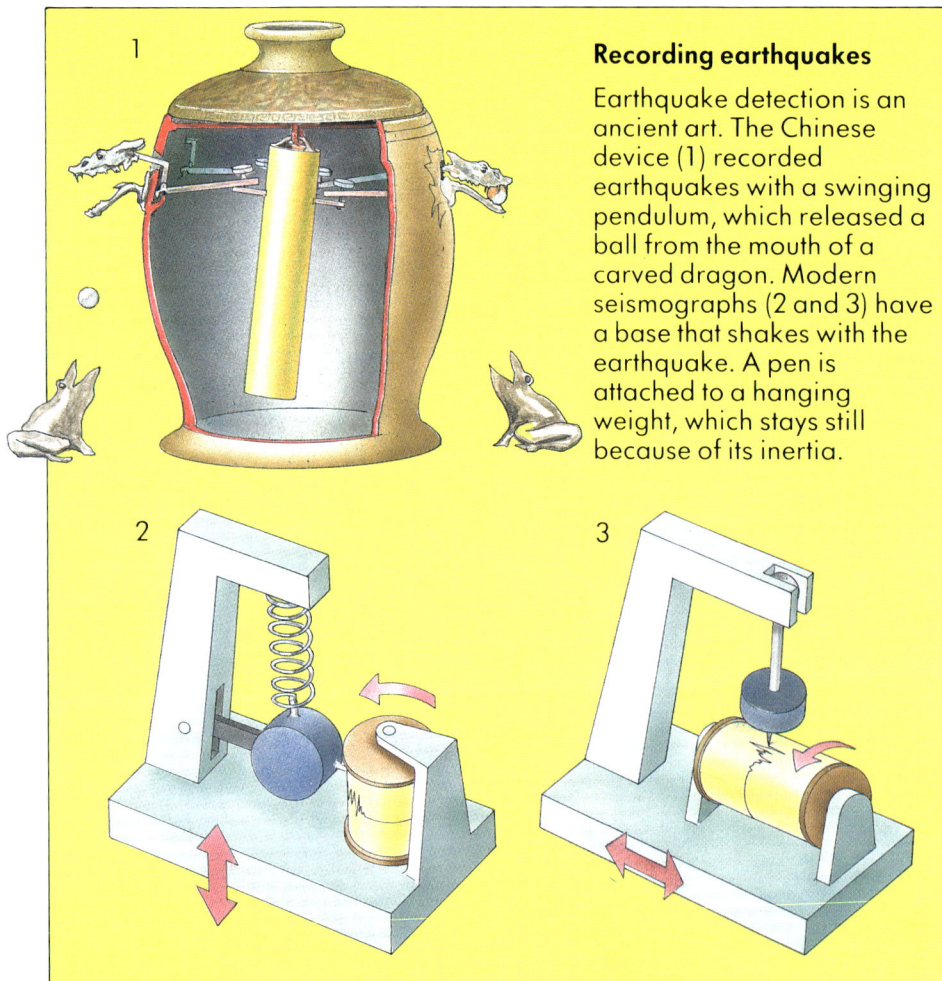

**Recording earthquakes**

Earthquake detection is an ancient art. The Chinese device (1) recorded earthquakes with a swinging pendulum, which released a ball from the mouth of a carved dragon. Modern seismographs (2 and 3) have a base that shakes with the earthquake. A pen is attached to a hanging weight, which stays still because of its inertia.

▶ The result of a severe earthquake that struck Mexico City in September 1985. A multistorey building has collapsed like a pack of cards. During this earthquake, more than 10,000 people died.

▼ The notorious San Andreas fault near San Bernardino in California. Movements along the fault cause frequent earthquakes.

# Rocks and minerals

## Spot facts

- The most common elements in the Earth's crust are oxygen and silicon, usually united as silica. Together they make up just over three-quarters of the crust.

- The oldest rocks are 3,800 million years old. They are found in Greenland.

- Chalk is the microscopic remains of tiny creatures that lived in the seas during the Cretaceous Period of Earth's history, 144-65 million years ago. "Cretaceous" means chalky.

- The rocks at the top of Mount Everest formed at the bottom of the sea 50 million years ago.

Several kinds of rocks make up the Earth's crust. They have formed in different ways: some from red-hot lava that spewed out of volcanoes, some from rock debris swept down from the mountains by rushing water and some from the fossils of ancient sea creatures. All the rocks are made up of collections of minerals, usually in the form of glassy crystals packed haphazardly together. But here and there, in cavities in the rocks, the crystals have room to grow into beautiful shapes. Well are they called "the flowers of the mineral kingdom".

▶ The Giant's Causeway in Northern Ireland is a basaltic lava flow 50 million years old. As it cooled and solidified, it split into the distinctive columns that make the site so famous.

# Reading the rocks

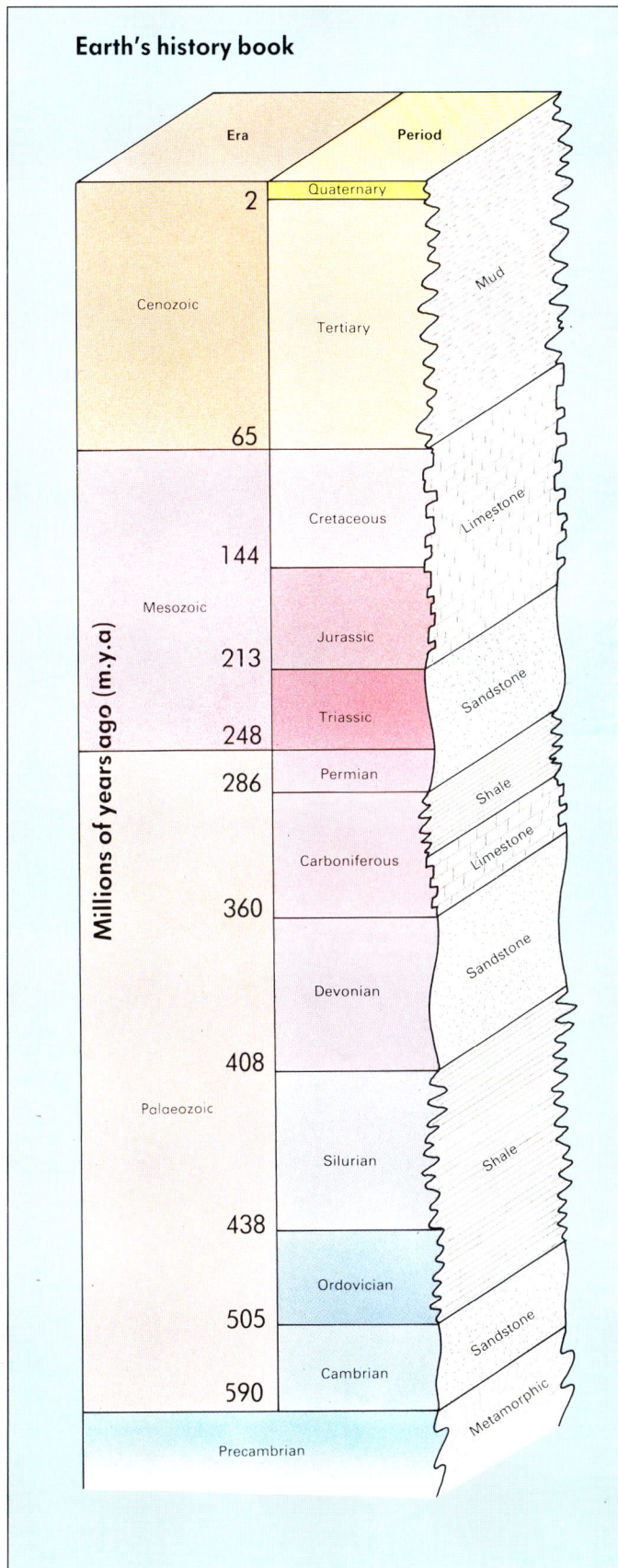

## Earth's history book

| Era | Period | |
|---|---|---|
| | | |

**Millions of years ago (m.y.a)**

| | |
|---|---|
| Cenozoic | 2 — Quaternary |
| | Tertiary |
| | 65 |
| Mesozoic | Cretaceous — 144 |
| | Jurassic — 213 |
| | Triassic — 248 |
| | Permian — 286 |
| | Carboniferous — 360 |
| Palaeozoic | Devonian — 408 |
| | Silurian — 438 |
| | Ordovician — 505 |
| | Cambrian — 590 |
| Precambrian | |

Rock types shown: Mud, Limestone, Sandstone, Shale, Limestone, Sandstone, Shale, Sandstone, Metamorphic

The Earth's crust consists of three types of rocks. When molten material from the Earth's interior solidifies, it forms igneous rock. When fragments of sand, silt or rubble are laid down, compressed and cemented into a solid mass, the result is a sedimentary rock. When pre-existing rocks are crushed and "cooked" deep within a mountain range their mineral content changes. The resulting rocks are termed metamorphic rocks.

Sedimentary rocks are most common at the Earth's surface, and by studying them we can find out much about what happened in the past. Sediments accumulate under specific conditions. So when we see a bed of sandstone with ripple marks in it, we can deduce that it was formed from a bed of sand laid down in a shallow sea. If, above it, there is a bed of mudstone containing the fossils of freshwater snails, we can deduce that a river later swept its muds into the area and covered the sand.

Examples like this have enabled us to write the full history of the Earth's surface from the days when sediments first began to form.

◀ Two centuries of studying the rocks has enabled geologists to work out a timescale of the Earth's history. Geological time is divided for convenience into a number of eras and periods.

▼ Fossils, such as these ammonites, can help to tell the age and the history of a rock, because the animals lived only during a particular period and under certain climatic conditions.

# Changing rocks

We just need to look around us at the conditions of the Earth's surface today to realize the range of conditions that must have existed in times past. We know that we get different kinds of sands in rivers, beaches and deserts. We see that streams produce silt, and lakes become choked with peat. Coarse shingle gathers on the shoreline. At the bottom of the sea muds and oozes, and fragments of seashell and coral accumulate. All these sediments eventually produce different sedimentary rocks.

Within these rocks there are different structures. Sand laid down in a river forms twisted beds that reflect the effects of the water current. The shapes of sand dunes can be seen in sandstones formed from desert sands. Coarse sediments form from particles deposited in strong currents, and fine sediments in gentle currents. Cracks develop in drying mud, and these can be preserved in the subsequent rocks. The study of this kind of evidence is the science of historical geology, also called stratigraphy.

**The rock cycle**

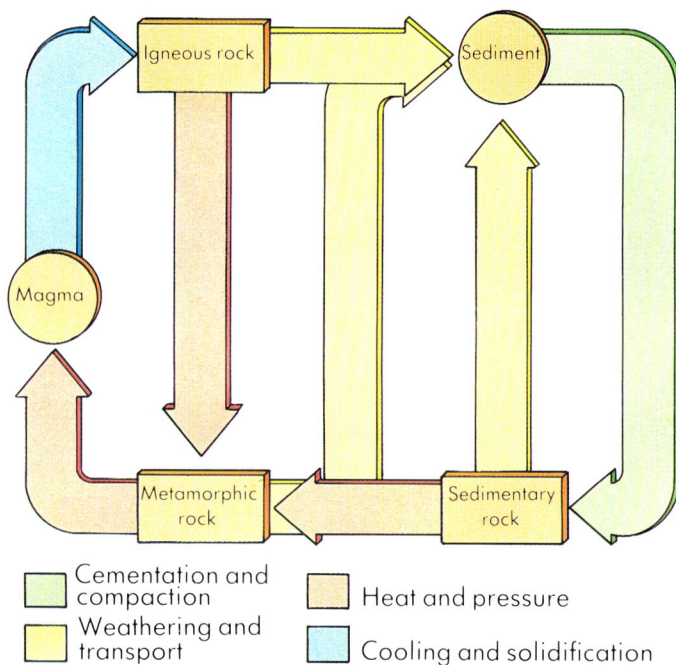

Cementation and compaction

Weathering and transport

Heat and pressure

Cooling and solidification

▲ Rocks are constantly being destroyed and recreated, a process known as the rock cycle. Many stages are involved. Sediments form sedimentary rock, which may later be crushed and re-formed in the heart of a mountain to produce metamorphic rock. The sedimentary rock may even melt with the heat and later solidify into igneous rock. All types may crumble when exposed, and their debris forms new sediments.

**Movement and deposition of sediments**

"The present is the key to the past," said pioneer geologist James Hutton in 1785. Using this idea, we can analyse sedimentary rocks and compare them with the many processes that are producing sediments today.

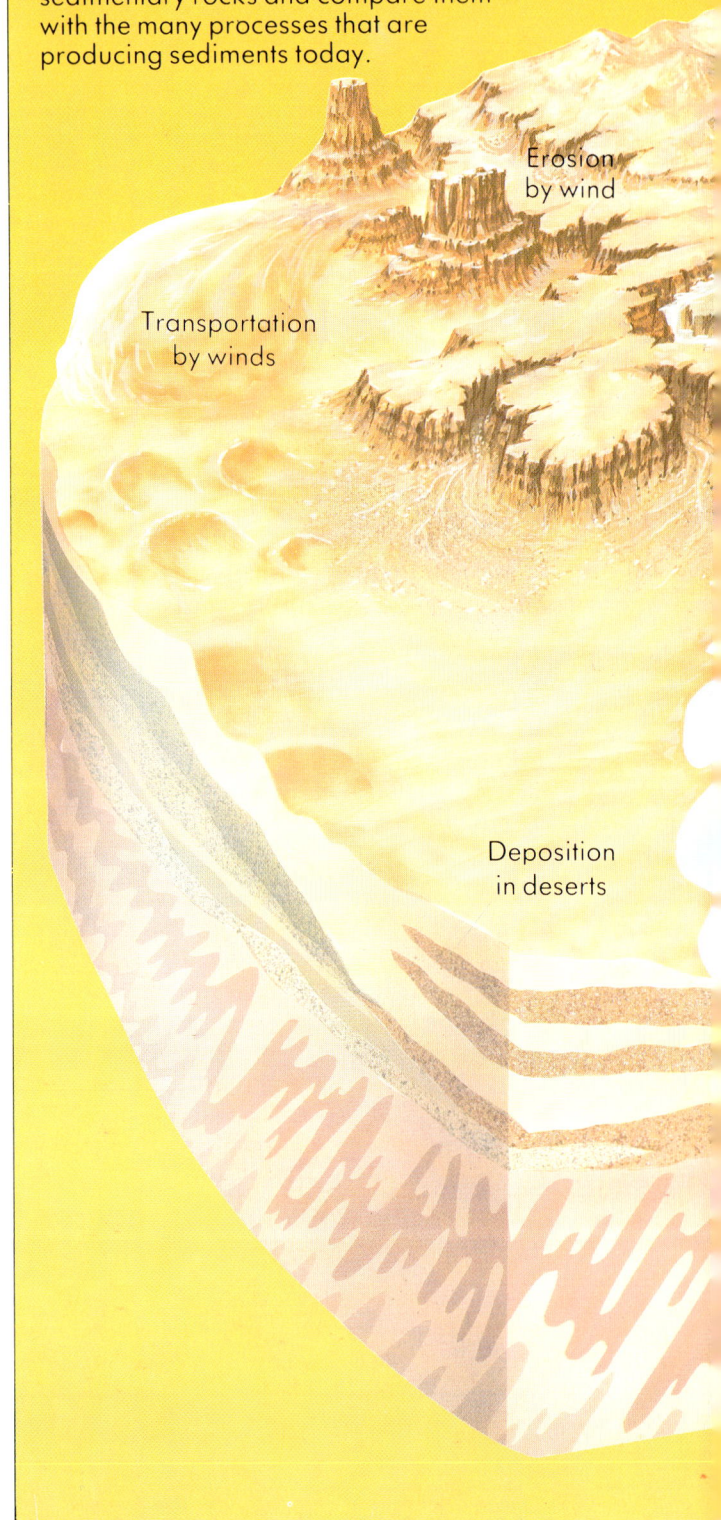

Erosion by wind

Transportation by winds

Deposition in deserts

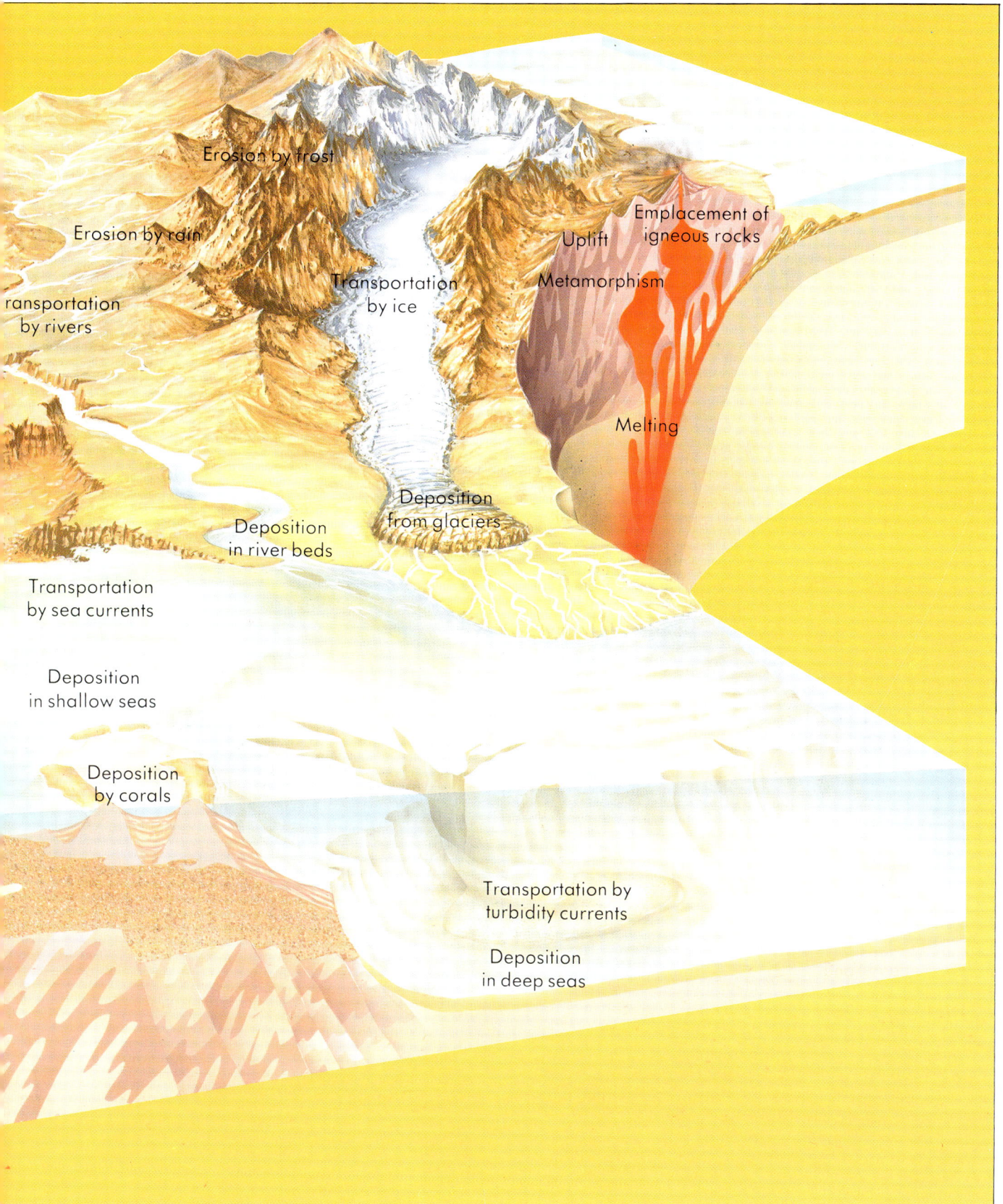

Erosion by frost

Erosion by rain

Transportation
by rivers

Transportation
by ice

Uplift

Emplacement of
igneous rocks

Metamorphism

Melting

Deposition
in river beds

Deposition
from glaciers

Transportation
by sea currents

Deposition
in shallow seas

Deposition
by corals

Transportation by
turbidity currents

Deposition
in deep seas

# Igneous rocks

Perhaps the simplest type of rock, and the most easily understood, is igneous rock. Its formation is theoretically quite straightforward. Molten material from inside the Earth cools and becomes a solid mass.

There are two main types of igneous rock – intrusive and extrusive. Intrusive rocks form when a mass of molten material is injected into the rocks of the crust and solidifies there without reaching the surface. We see intrusive igneous rocks only when the rocks above have been eroded away. Extrusive rocks form when the molten material cools on the surface, as for instance in a lava flow.

Intrusive rocks cool very slowly, and so they tend to be coarse-grained. The crystals of individual minerals are big enough to be seen by the naked eye. Granite is a good example. Extrusive rocks cool quickly and so are fine-grained. They have microscopic mineral crystals. Basalt is an example. Sometimes the molten rock begins to cool underground and the

first minerals form large crystals. Then the whole lot bursts out at the surface and solidifies quickly. The result is a rock called a porphyry, which consists of a fine groundmass with big crystals embedded in it.

## Composition of igneous rocks

Igneous rocks are also classified by their composition. This is rarely the same as the original magma, the molten material from the Earth's interior. The magma is rich in the chemical silica and forms silicate minerals.

As the molten material rises through the Earth's crust and begins to cool, some minerals crystallize out before the others. The silicate minerals olivine and pyroxine are early crystallizers. These, which are rich in iron and magnesium, sink to the bottom of an intrusion. Silicate minerals such as feldspars and micas, which are low in iron and magnesium but rich in the lighter metals potassium and sodium, tend to solidify later. Uncombined silica forms the

◀ ▼ The wrinkled, ropy surface is typical of basalt, a most common extrusive basic igneous rock. After lava erupts from a volcano, it may flow for some distance over the ground as a river of fire. During this time its surface cools and hardens. The chilled surface is dragged along by the movement of the liquid beneath, and it twists and distorts as it goes. The ropy lava is known by its Hawaiian name of aa. The islands of Iceland and Hawaii were built up from the seabed by successive layers of lava flows like these.

mineral quartz. As a result, dark iron-rich rocks form deep down, whereas light-coloured silica-rich rocks form closer to the surface. Geologists call the darker rocks basic and the lighter rocks acidic.

Igneous rocks that form from magma being brought up at a constructive plate margin tend to be basic. Coarse intrusive dolerite and fine extrusive basalt are formed there. At a destructive plate margin, the magma is made of molten plate material and is usually richer in silica. The rocks that form there tend to be acidic igneous rocks, such as intrusive granite and extrusive andesite.

Although the silicate minerals are rich in metals, it is difficult to remove the metals from the silica. They are therefore no good as ores. Silicate minerals are thus referred to as the rock-forming minerals. Ore minerals – used as sources of metals – are usually sulphides or oxides of metals, and they do not usually form the bulk of the rock.

▶ Sheer granite cliff-faces provide a spectacular sight. El Capitan cliff in Yosemite National Park shows little sign so far of any erosion.

▼ Granite is a typical intrusive igneous rock. Its feldspar minerals break down easily on exposure to air, and so exposed granite wears away into rounded lumps.

# Sedimentary rocks

The rocks which are formed when a layer of mud, sand or other natural debris is compressed and cemented together are called sedimentary rocks. Like igneous rocks, they can be classified according to their origin. The main type is clastic sedimentary rock. This is formed from fragments of other rocks, such as sand or shingle.

Any rock that is exposed at the surface of the Earth is worn away by the relentless onslaught of the wind and rain. Some of its minerals, such as feldspar, may be dissolved away by acid in rainwater. Or the rock may be broken apart by the expansion of ice in its cracks. All these actions make rock break down into fragments that can be washed away by streams or even blown away by the wind. Eventually the fragments settle. The coarsest fragments do not travel far, but come to rest as boulders, cobbles and shingle at the foot of a cliff or on a shoreline. Finer pieces like sand and silt can be carried farther and deposited on beaches or seabeds. The finest matter is washed well out to sea and settles as mud. These various sediments may eventually become sedimentary rocks such as conglomerate, sandstone and shale.

The second classification is biogenic sedimentary rock. It is formed from fragments of once-living matter, such as corals or seashells. These form limestones in which you can often see the fossils of the creatures that originally formed them.

▼ The sand in the foreground may eventually become sandstone like that in the background. This will only happen once the sands are buried, compressed and cemented together. Then the sandstone will appear at the surface only if the whole area is caught up in mountain-building activity, and the overlying beds are worn away. The beds that were once horizontal will be tilted up and twisted. They may be distorted by bends called folds, or they may shift along cracks called faults.

▲ Cheddar Gorge, England, is formed of limestone. This is a very common sedimentary rock that occurs in distinct layers or beds. They may either be very thin or very thick.

Finally, chemical sedimentary rock forms when substances dissolved in the water come out of solution and form a crust on the bottom of a lake or the sea. Rock salt and certain kinds of limestones form in this way when lakes and shallow seas dry up.

## Natural concrete

When sediments are buried, they are compressed beneath the weight of the sediments on top of them. Then groundwater seeps through them, depositing mineral crystals on and between the fragments. This cements them together, just like cement holds together the gravel and sand in concrete, and turns the loose material into a hard, solid mass.

▲ Some sedimentary rocks have practical uses. The coal being mined here is a biogenic sedimentary rock made from ancient vegetation. Many sandstones and limestones make good building materials.

## Sedimentary rock types

We can usually identify a sedimentary rock type by looking at the fragments that make it up. A chemical sedimentary rock, such as rock salt (1), is made up of crystals, rather like those in an igneous rock. A clastic sedimentary rock, such as the conglomerate (2), consists of distinct lumps. The lumps may be rounded if they have been washed about for a long time, or jagged and angular if they have not travelled far. They may also be coarse or fine. In a biogenic sedimentary rock, such as chalk (3), we can see the fragments of shells. The example shown here is of a microscopic fossil, but often the shell fragments can be seen with the naked eye.

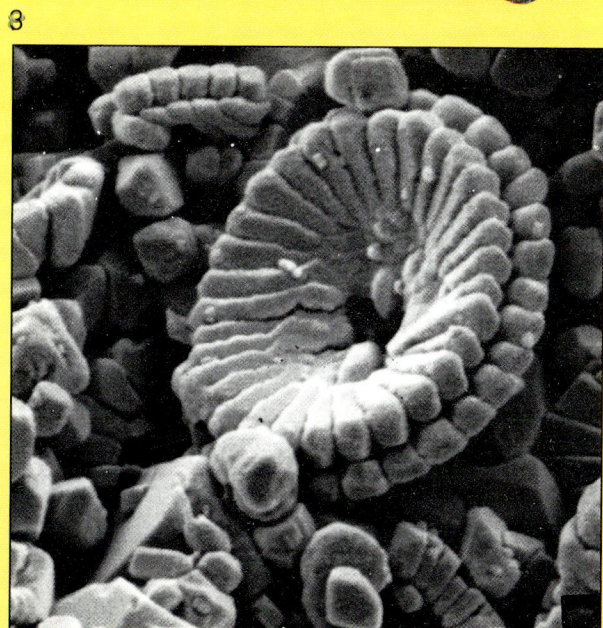

# Metamorphic rocks

When the drifting continents grind into each other, the immense pressures involved crumple up mountains and alter the rocks deep inside the crust. When a rock is subjected to so much pressure and heat that its minerals change, the rock becomes a metamorphic rock. But the rock remains solid throughout this process. If it melts and then solidifies again, it changes into an igneous rock.

Geologists recognize two main types of metamorphic rock. The first is thermal metamorphic rock. This is formed principally by heat. It is usually found in localized patches around igneous intrusions, where the heat of the intrusion has re-formed the surrounding rock. A thermal metamorphic rock can be difficult to distinguish from an igneous rock, because it tends to consist of masses of inter-grown crystals with little recognizable pattern.

Thermal metamorphic rocks, however, contain minerals found in no other type of rock.

The second type of metamorphic rock is formed by pressure. The roots of whole mountain chains can be altered in this way. For this reason, the rock is called regional metamorphic rock. Slate is an example. The new minerals that form may do so in contorted layers and bands, corresponding to the direction of the pressure. The very ancient terrains in the centres of continents are usually formed from regional metamorphic rocks.

▼ A slate quarry. Slate is a fine-grained regional metamorphic rock, and one of the few that is economically valuable. The pressure that formed it produced new crystals of mica, all aligned in the same direction. Mica crystals form sheets, and for this reason slate easily splits into thin slices that can be used for covering roofs and for other purposes.

## Colourful crystals

Individual minerals can be difficult to identify just by looking at them with the naked eye. Colour is not a good guide, because any mineral can contain traces of an impurity that changes the colour completely. Quartz, for instance, can be transparent, milky white, pink or brown. Corundum, an aluminium oxide, can be discoloured red, which would make it a ruby; or blue, which would make it a sapphire.

However, the "streak" of a mineral is quite distinctive. If a sample of mineral is scraped over a hard surface, it leaves a streak of fine powder. The colour of that powder is constant for a particular mineral whatever impurity it may contain.

Crystal form is a good indicator, but usually in a rock the crystals are crammed together and show no good shape.

A useful test is hardness. Some minerals are harder than others and can be tested by scratching a sample against others of known hardness. A mineral scratches only a mineral that is softer than it is. Quartz is quite a hard mineral, and it scratches softer minerals such as calcite, but can itself be scratched only by even harder minerals such as corundum.

Lustre and the effect of fracture can both be seen. When light catches the mineral, it may have a glassy, metallic or dull lustre. When it is broken, the broken face may be straight, ragged or shell-like. The appearance helps to identify the mineral.

A geologist uses a special microscope to examine a thin slice of rock and identify its minerals. The rock slice is ground until it is paper-thin and transparent. The specimen is examined using polarized light, which produces distinctive coloured patterns when it passes through a mineral.

Key
1 Pyrites, with a metallic lustre.
2 Flint, with a conchoidal, or shell-like, fracture.
3 Rock salt, with good crystal shape.
4 Quartz, with a brown impurity.
5 Diamond, the hardest mineral of all.

Minerals may be identified by their lustre, by the way they fracture, by the shapes of their crystals, or by their hardness.

# The changing landscape

"As old as the hills" is an expression that we use when we think of something as being very old indeed. Yet compared with the age of the Earth the hills may not be so very ancient. The Himalayas, the greatest mountain chain on Earth, are less than 50 million years old, and that is not a great span of time in geological terms. Whenever a rock becomes exposed at the surface of the Earth, and whenever an area of land rises above sea level, natural forces begin to destroy it. Gravity, running water, wind, rain, sea and frost all work together to erode, or wear down, the landscape back to sea level. The face of the Earth is also changing because of human activity.

▶ In Monument Valley, Utah, there are wide extents of thick, horizontally-bedded sandstones that have been attacked and worn away. They have been eroded by wind and rain. Everywhere we look, we can see similar changes that have taken place in the landscape.

# River erosion

Much of the carving up of the landscape is done by water, and particularly by rivers. Rainwater that soaks into the ground often returns to the surface as a spring. From the spring it runs downhill as a stream.

In this young stage of a river, the water runs quickly. The faster a river flows, the more erosive power it has. It tends to erode away its bed, cutting a deep V-shaped gully as it goes. Rocks and stones picked up by the moving water are bounced along the stream bed, adding to the erosive force. Waterfalls and rapids are common at this stage.

When it leaves the hilly areas and begins to flow down a more gentle slope, the river reaches what is known as its mature stage. It still erodes the landscape but it also deposits some of the material that it has been carrying downwards. River valleys tend to be broad at this stage, much broader than the river itself. Over the years, the river's course moves about the valley floor. As a river flows round a curve, it moves more quickly on the outside. The bank at this side is undercut and worn back. On the inside of the curve the current is slower and the debris that has been carried tends to be deposited there as a beach.

The final stage of the river can be thought of as its old age. There is no valley and the water has no power to erode. It moves slowly across a plain, depositing material as it goes. Eventually it reaches the sea.

▲ A typical feature of a mountain stream is white, foaming water. It is the youthful stage of a river. It is the time when the river runs fastest and is at its most violent. It bounces over rapids and waterfalls, scouring out its narrow bed. The fast-flowing river picks up rocks and gravel and carries them along towards the lowlands. By the time it reaches the sea it is moving slowly.

### Lazy river

Meanders are loops in a slow-flowing river (1). They form during a river's old age. Curves tend to get bigger by eroding the outer bank and building up the inner one (2). The result is a river that swings across a flat plain of deposited sediment, like England's River Cuckmere (3). A meander may be cut off to form an ox-bow lake.

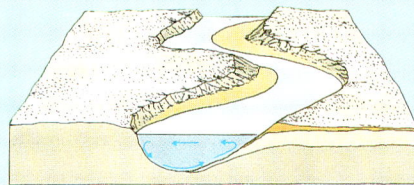

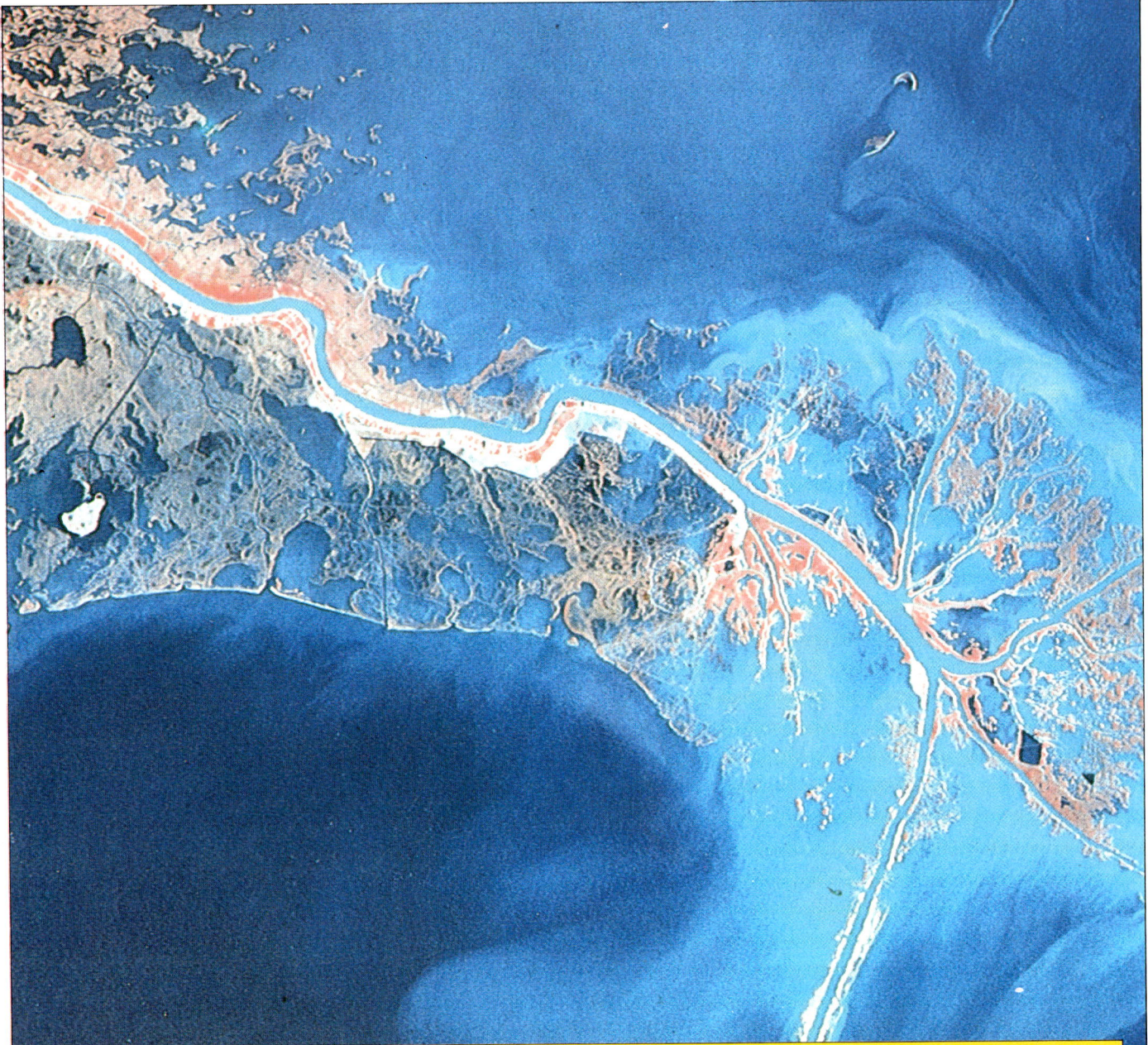

# Weathering

### Deltas

A river ends at its mouth. If there are few sea currents at that point, the debris builds up to form a delta. The delta can build out as banks along a series of channels, as in the Mississippi River (above and 1). Or it can spread out to form a semicircular area of triangular islands, as in the deltas of the River Nile (2) and the River Niger (3).

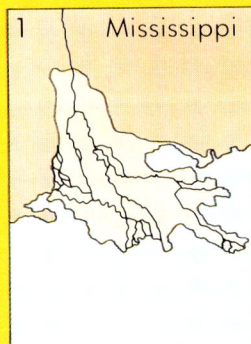

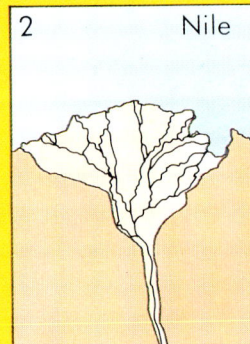

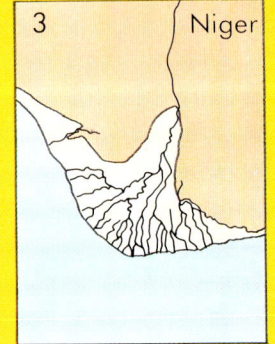

1 Mississippi
2 Nile
3 Niger

Much of the debris that falls into rivers and gets washed away has been broken from exposed rocks. This has been done by the erosive action of both wind and rain, water and ice.

Rainwater, even without the addition of pollution, is quite acidic. As moisture condenses from the clouds and falls in the form of drops, it dissolves carbon dioxide gas from the atmosphere. It then becomes weak carbonic acid. On soaking into the ground, the acid reacts with particular minerals in the rocks. This is very noticeable in granite areas, where the feldspars in the granite are attacked and turned into soft clay minerals. The other minerals in the granite – quartz and mica – then fall loose and are carried away as sand. This is why many granite areas have china clay pits and dazzling white quartz beaches.

The other type of rock mainly affected by the acidity of rainwater is limestone. Limestone is composed almost entirely of the mineral calcite, which dissolves in weak acids. The water flowing through the rock dissolves it to form galleries and caverns. Within them, the water redeposits the dissolved calcite as stalactites and stalagmites. The calcite is also redeposited in kettles and water pipes, giving the problem known as hard water.

The rocks of dry areas also have trouble with the weather. The wind in the desert can pick up sand particles and hurl them against exposed rocks and cliff-faces. This wears them away in a natural "sandblasting" effect, and produces yet more sand that can erode more rock. The infrequent rains that do fall in the desert soak into the surface layers of exposed rocks. This breaks down the minerals near the surface, and weakens the outermost skin. During the hot days and cold nights these surface layers expand and contract, and eventually split away to produce what is called onion-skin weathering. The rock comes apart layer by layer and leaves the core in the form of a rounded hill called an inselberg.

**Features of a cave**

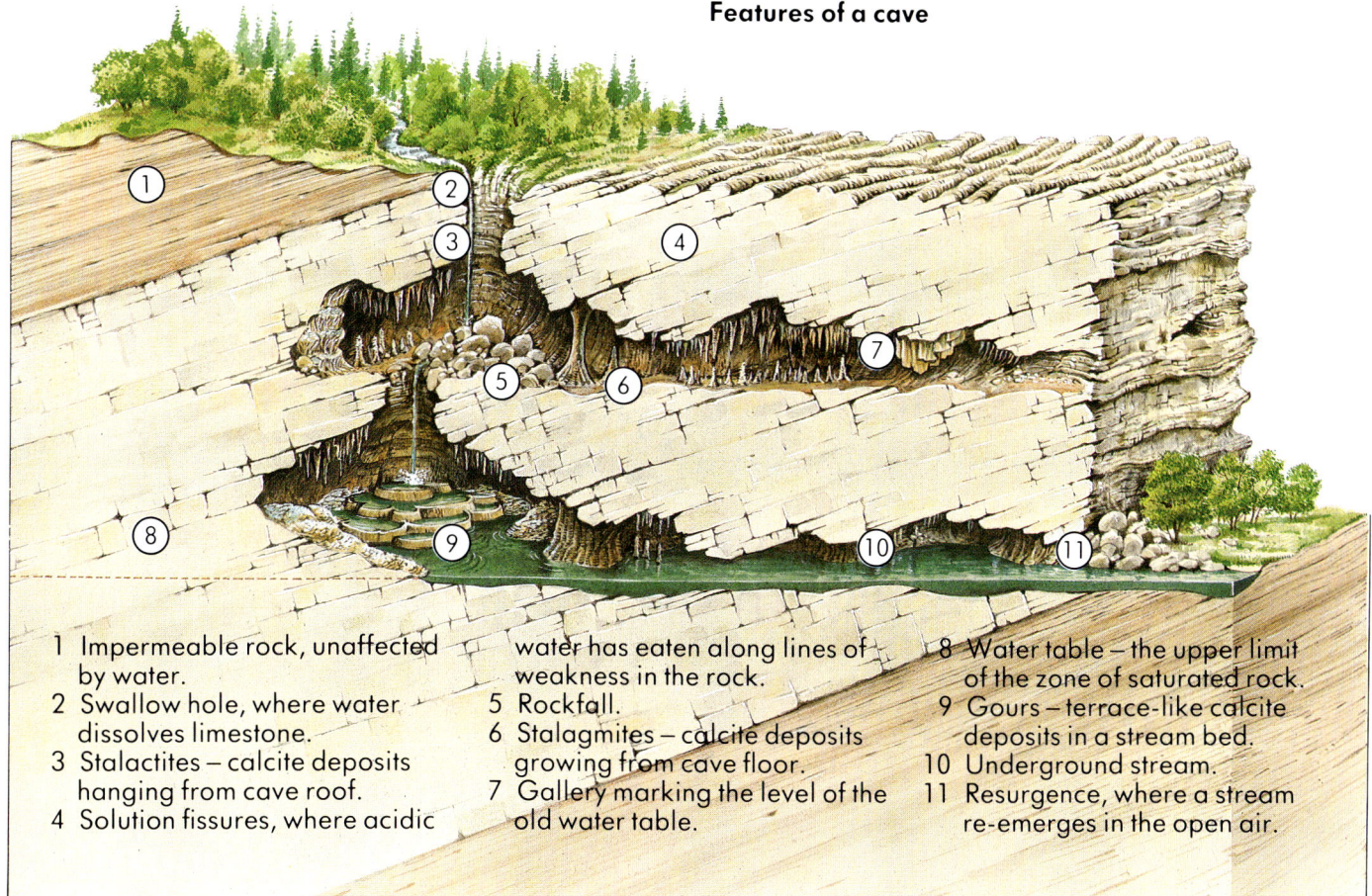

1 Impermeable rock, unaffected by water.
2 Swallow hole, where water dissolves limestone.
3 Stalactites – calcite deposits hanging from cave roof.
4 Solution fissures, where acidic water has eaten along lines of weakness in the rock.
5 Rockfall.
6 Stalagmites – calcite deposits growing from cave floor.
7 Gallery marking the level of the old water table.
8 Water table – the upper limit of the zone of saturated rock.
9 Gours – terrace-like calcite deposits in a stream bed.
10 Underground stream.
11 Resurgence, where a stream re-emerges in the open air.

# Ice and frost

An ever-present problem in the northern winter is the possibility of water pipes freezing. When they do, they crack and split because of the expansion of the ice inside. Exactly the same thing happens in nature. On icy mountains water soaks into pores and cracks in exposed rocks. When it freezes, the water turns to ice. The ice expands with a pressure that widens the pores and cracks, splitting the rocks apart and breaking up entire mountainsides. Masses of broken blocks that slope downwards from craggy peaks are a result of this destructive action. They are called scree slopes.

A similar mechanism brings stones to the surface of a garden in winter time. Water beneath a buried stone freezes more readily than that in the soil around because the stone absorbs its heat more quickly. Ice forming beneath the stone expands and pushes the stone upwards. In permanently cold regions the whole soil surface is raised in a regular series of low humps. The stones brought to the surface collect in the troughs between the humps and produce a honeycomb-like pattern.

Ice can break and change rocks. It can also transport things. A glacier is a mass of ice that moves slowly under the influence of gravity. It is one of the strongest agents of transportation that there is. Much of the landscape of the Northern Hemisphere is formed from debris deposited by continent-wide glaciers during the ice ages of the last two million years.

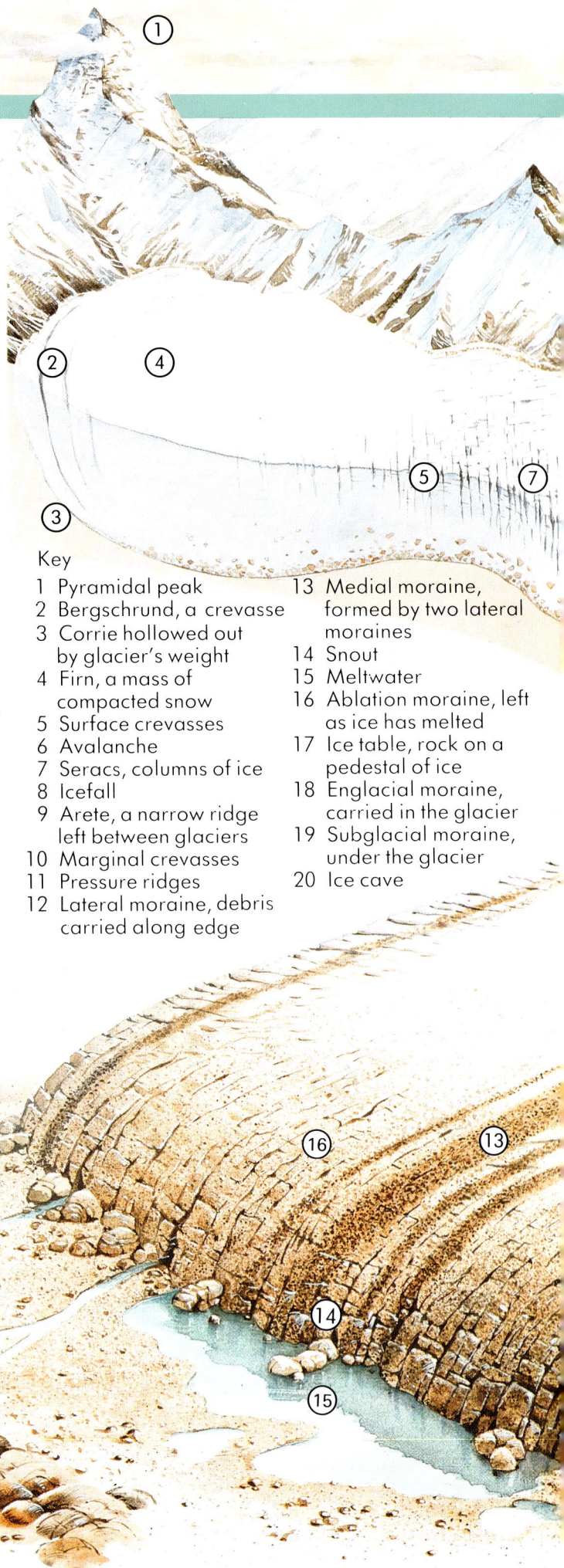

## Key

1  Pyramidal peak
2  Bergschrund, a crevasse
3  Corrie hollowed out by glacier's weight
4  Firn, a mass of compacted snow
5  Surface crevasses
6  Avalanche
7  Seracs, columns of ice
8  Icefall
9  Arete, a narrow ridge left between glaciers
10  Marginal crevasses
11  Pressure ridges
12  Lateral moraine, debris carried along edge
13  Medial moraine, formed by two lateral moraines
14  Snout
15  Meltwater
16  Ablation moraine, left as ice has melted
17  Ice table, rock on a pedestal of ice
18  Englacial moraine, carried in the glacier
19  Subglacial moraine, under the glacier
20  Ice cave

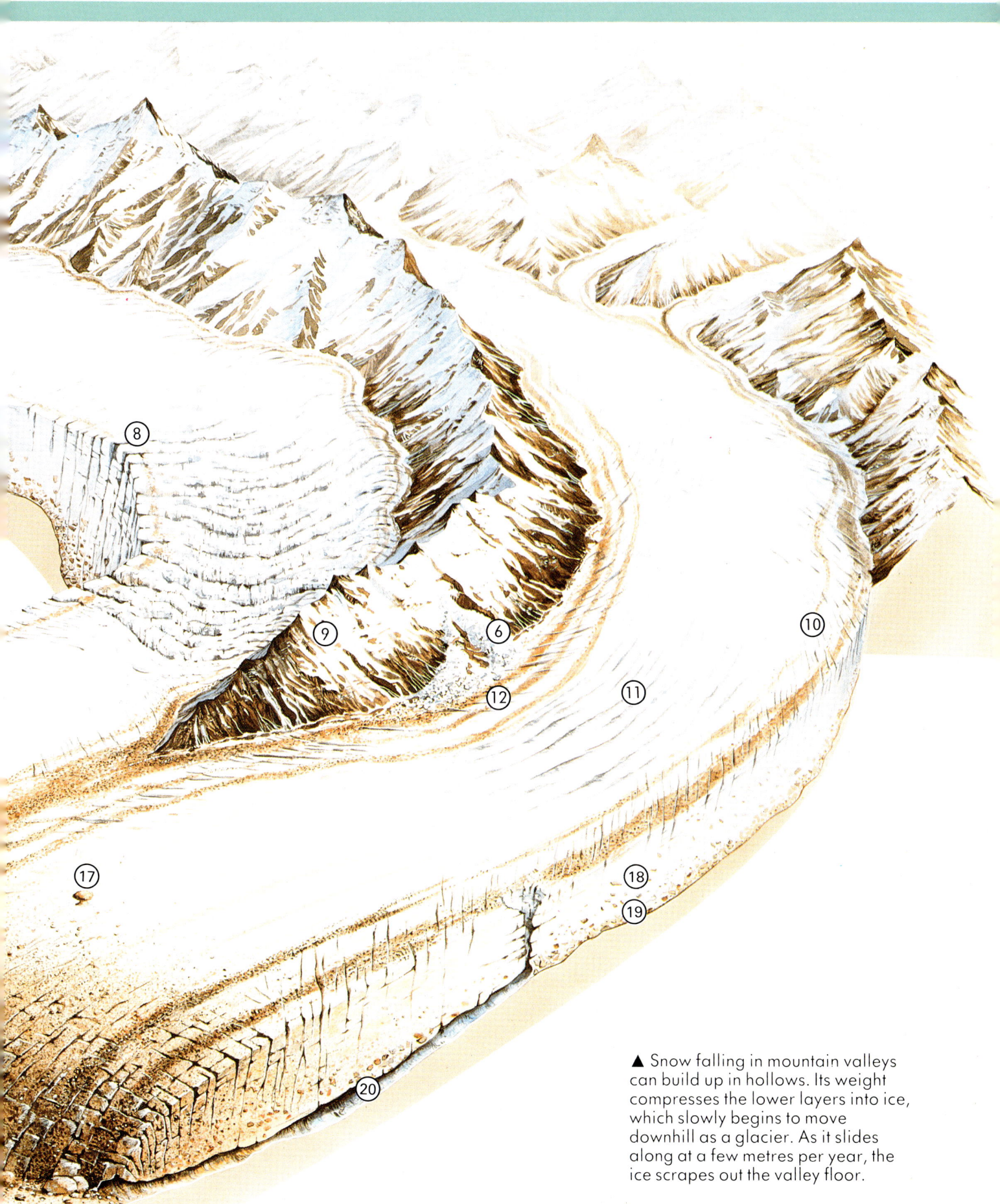

▲ Snow falling in mountain valleys can build up in hollows. Its weight compresses the lower layers into ice, which slowly begins to move downhill as a glacier. As it slides along at a few metres per year, the ice scrapes out the valley floor.

# The changing scene

The landscape is never static. It changes from day to day, year to year, millenium to millenium. Most of these changes are natural. But with the coming of civilization, many have been caused by the activity of people.

Almost everything that civilization does has an impact on the surface of the Earth. About 5,000 years ago irrigation was first practised in the Middle East. Rivers were diverted to make dry desert areas fertile. The first cities were built, and these were often constructed on artificial hills, for defence. The people of low-lying lands by shallow seas often extend their farmland by walling off areas of sea and draining them. The Dutch have been doing this since the 7th century. Since the Industrial Revolution of the 18th century, vast areas of the landscape have been dug up for raw materials.

More spectacular are the unintentional changes in the landscape caused by human activities. Building breakwaters for harbours, or removing beach shingle for building, can alter sea currents. As a result, local seafronts can be washed away. Bad farming practices can alter the structure of the soil so that it falls apart and is washed away or blown away in the wind. In this way, fertile farmland can turn to desert very quickly.

With the population increasing every year, the impact that civilization has on the environment becomes greater and more significant all the time.

▼ The world's biggest hole in the ground is the Bingham Canyon Copper Mine in Utah. It has a depth of 774 m and covers an area of 7.21 sq km.

▲ In deserts, sand is blown along close to the ground at a height of about 1 m. It hits the base of rocks, eroding them into mushroom shapes.

▶ The sea is constantly eating away at the coastline. It undercuts cliffs and erodes headlands into isolated pillars of rock called stacks.

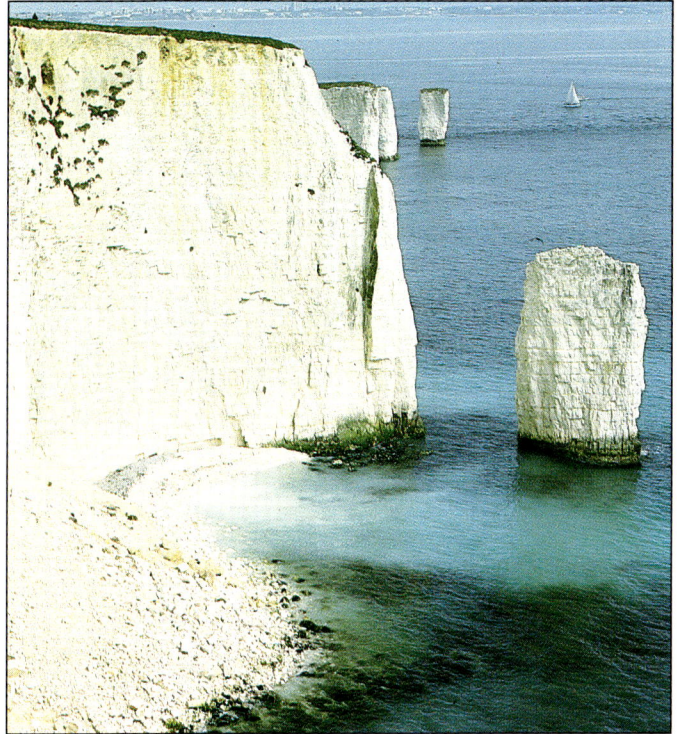

## Igneous landforms

The shape of the landscape depends mainly on the type of rock it is made from. When an igneous rock fills a large crack, the structure is called a dyke. As the surrounding rocks are worn away, the dyke juts up like a wall across the scenery. An igneous rock forming a layer between beds of a sedimentary rock forms a structure called a sill. When this is eroded, it may look like a thick, hard sedimentary bed.

Sometimes the magma rising up a crack stops at a particular level and domes up the sedimentary rocks above it. This produces a laccolith, sometimes seen on the surface as a ring-like structure in the uplifted sedimentary rocks. When an ancient volcano is worn away, the solid igneous material in the vent may remain standing as a pinnacle (below), showing where the volcano once stood.

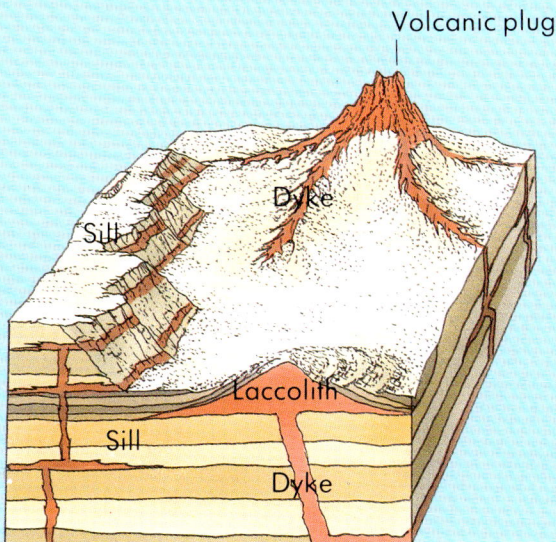

Volcanic plug
Dyke
Sill
Laccolith
Sill
Dyke

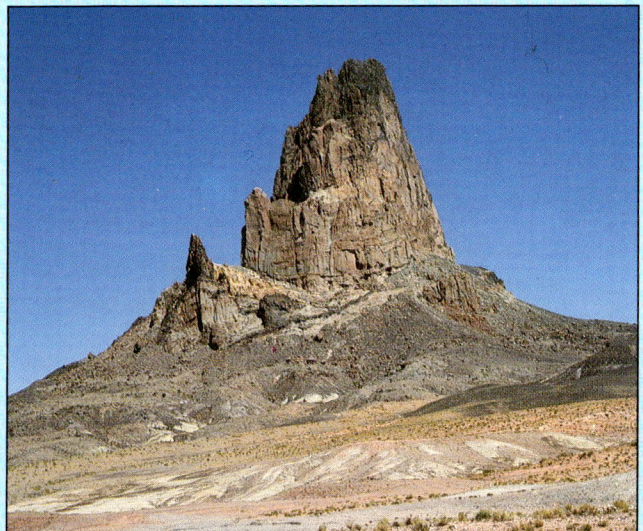

# Glossary

**acidic** In geological terms, an igneous rock that contains a high proportion of silica. It has nothing to do with acidity in the chemical sense.

**ammonite** An extinct animal that resembled an octopus in a coiled shell. Fossils of ammonites are common in marine sedimentary rocks of the Mesozoic era.

**aquifer** A water-bearing bed of rock.

**artesian** A well or a spring from which water gushes up under its own pressure.

**asthenosphere** A soft layer within the Earth's mantle on which the solid lithosphere moves.

**axis** The imaginary line through the Earth, or any other body, around which it spins.

**basic** In geological terms, a rock that contains a low proportion of silica.

**biogenic** A term that describes a form of sedimentary rock. Biogenic sedimentary rock is rock formed from fragments of once-living matter, such as shells or wood.

**block mountain** An upland bounded by faults along which it was raised, or along which the surrounding landscape has subsided.

**Cenozoic** The era of geological time spanning from 65 million years ago up until the present day.

**chemical** A term that describes a form of sedimentary rock. Chemical sedimentary rock is rock formed from a solution, such as salt.

**clastic** A term that describes a form of sedimentary rock. Clastic sedimentary rock is rock formed from fragments worn off other rocks.

**continent** A large continuous landmass that rises above the ocean floor. Most geologists accept that there are seven continents. Asia,

Europe, Africa, South America, North America, Australia and Antarctica.

**continental drift** The phenomenon in which the continents appear to have moved throughout geological time. Such movements are now accounted for by plate tectonics.

**core** The innermost part of the Earth's structure.

**corrie** A bowl-shaped hollow from which a glacier flows. It is widened and deepened by the weight of the glacier itself. When the glacier melts, it often leaves a corrie lake.

**crust** The outermost part of the Earth's structure.

**crystal** A regular, naturally formed shape, usually with flat faces and sharp edges. Most substances will form crystals, the shape of which reflects their chemical structure.

**dyke** An igneous intrusion consisting of rock cutting across the bedding of the country rock. A dyke is formed as a crack fills up with magma.

**epicentre** The point on the Earth's surface directly above the focus of an earthquake.

**erosion** The process whereby the rocks and soils of the surface of the Earth are broken down by the action of the weather, by streams, by glaciers or by human interference.

**extrusive** Term that describes a form of igneous rock. Extrusive igneous rock is rock that breaks through the Earth's surface before it solidifies.

**fault** A crack in the Earth's crusts along which it has moved, caused by tectonic movements.

**focus** The point at which most movement occurs in an earthquake.

**fold** A bend in the rocks caused by tectonic movements.

**fold mountain** A mountain or a mountain range formed by folding, usually as tectonic plates move against one another.

**fossil** The remains or trace of a once-living organism preserved in the rocks.

**geology** The study of the Earth, its rocks and minerals, its fossils and its changing conditions throughout time.

**glacier** A mass of ice, formed from compacted snow, that moves by its own weight down a valley.

**groundwater** Water that is held in the rocks and soils of the Earth.

**hard water** Water that contains a high concentration of dissolved calcium carbonate. Such water produces mineral deposits in kettles and pipes.

**historical geology** That aspect of geology that describes the conditions in past times from analysis of the rocks formed at that time.

**ice age** A period of time in which the climate is colder than normal and glaciers are particularly widespread. The most famous is that which took place in the last 2 million years, but there have been several throughout geological time.

**igneous rock** One that has formed as molten material, and has cooled and solidified, either on the Earth's surface – a volcanic or extrusive rock, or underground – an intrusive rock.

**inselberg** A rounded mass of rock protruding above an arid plain. It is a result of onion-skin weathering.

**intrusion** A body of igneous rock that has formed underground.

**laccolith** An intrusion which forces the sedimentary rock above it to form a dome shape.

**lava** Molten rocky material that

erupts from a volcano and solidifies on the Earth's surface.

**lithosphere** The solid proportion of the Earth's surface. It consists of the crust and the topmost part of the mantle. The tectonic plates of the Earth's surface are sections of the lithosphere.

**magma** Molten rocky material beneath the Earth's surface.

**magnetism** A property of certain metals that causes attraction and repulsion. The field (the space in which the effect is felt) has two ends, called the north pole and the south pole. When two magnetic objects are brought together, the unlike poles attract one another and the like poles repel. An electric current can produce a magnetic effect.

**mantle** The stony section of the Earth between the crust and the core.

**Mesozoic** The era in geological time that lasted between 248 and 65 million years ago.

**metamorphic rock** Rock that has been heated and/or crushed so much by the movements of the Earth that the components have recrystallized into new minerals.

**mineral** A naturally formed inorganic substance with a consistent chemical composition. All rocks are made up of an aggregation of minerals.

**moraine** Rocky debris scraped up and carried along by a glacier. Once the glacier has melted, the moraine forms landscape features.

**ore mineral** A mineral that contains a valuable metal which can be extracted economically.

**Palaeozoic** The era in geological time between 590 and 248 million years ago.

**plate tectonics** The movement of the Earth's surface, caused by the generation of new plate material at ocean ridges, its spreading, and its destruction in ocean trenches. This worldwide movement takes in the old concept of continental drift and the newer concept of seafloor spreading.

**regional** A term that describes a form of metamorphic rock. Regional metamorphic rock is rock formed by tectonic pressure.

**rift valley** A valley produced as an area of rock subsides between two faults, or folds downwards against a single fault.

**rock** In geological terms a rock is any substance that makes up the surface of the Earth, and includes consolidated sediments and soil. More commonly it refers to solid matter formed of minerals that have grown in a mass or have become cemented together.

**rock cycle** The process by which a rock forms. It is either lifted up by tectonic forces, then broken down by erosion, and the resulting fragments are consolidated into a new rock. Or alternatively the original rock melts and solidifies into a new rock.

**rock-forming mineral** A mineral that makes up the bulk of a rock and contains no useful metals that can be extracted.

**seafloor spreading** The phenomenon whereby the ocean floor is observed to become older farther away from the ocean ridges. The discovery was made in the 1960s and is now covered by the all-embracing concept of plate tectonics.

**sediment** Any loose material deposited in layers by water or wind.

**sedimentary rock** One that has formed as loose sediments have become compacted and cemented together.

**seismograph** A device for detecting hand measuring earthquakes.

**serac** A pinnacle of ice formed on a glacier where two sets of crevasses intersect.

**SIAL** Scientific shorthand for the substance of the continental crust. It is an abbreviation of the major constituents, **SI**licon and **AL**uminium.

**silicate** A mineral that contains silicon, oxygen and usually some other element. Silicates are the most common rock-forming minerals.

**sill** An igneous intrusion, consisting of a sheet of rock lying parallel to the bedding of the other rocks of the area.

**SIMA** Scientific shorthand for the substance of the oceanic crust. It is an abbreviation of the major constituents, **SI**licon and **MA**gnesium.

**stalactite** A hanging structure in a cave formed by the build-up of calcite from drops of water on the cave roof.

**stalagmite** A build-up of calcite on a cave floor, formed by the calcite coming out of solution from drops of water hitting the floor.

**tectonics** The study of the forces that move rocks, the movements themselves, and the structures, such as faults and folds, that are so formed.

**thermal** A term used to describe a form of metamorphic rock. Thermal metamorphic rock is formed by very high temperatures.

**vent** A fissure or a tunnel in a volcano, through which lava or gas emerges.

**volcano** A vent in the Earth's surface, from which lava and gas are expelled from the interior. The solidified lava around the vent usually builds up into a mountain.

**water table** The upper boundary of the underground zone in which the rocks are saturated with water.

# Index

## Further Reading

*The Young Scientist's Guide to the Physical World* by Jill Bailey and Tony Seddon (Oxford University Press, 1988)
*Volcanoes and Earthquakes* by Basil Booth (Wayland, 1988)
*Earth Facts* by L. Bresler (Usborne, 1986)
*Earthquake* by Bryce Walker (Time-Life, 1987)
*The Story of the Earth* by Peter Cattermole and Patrick Moore (Cambridge University Press, 1985)
*Rocks, Minerals and Fossils* by Keith Lye (Wayland, 1988)
*The Spread of Deserts* by Ewan McLeish (Wayland, 1989)
*The Science of the Earth* by Tom Williamson (Macmillan, 1984)
*The Earth* by Terry Jennings (Oxford University Press, 1988)

## Picture Credits